Keto-Mediterranean Diet Cookbook for Rapid Weight Loss

Recipe Book for Improved Brain Memory and Wellness Formula Health + Daily Planner Bonus

By Mia Breeze

Preface 7

CHAPTER 1 *Introduction to the Keto-Mediterranean Diet: The Best of Both Worlds 9*

CHAPTER 2 *Understanding Ketosis: The Dietary Engine of the Ketogenic Diet 19*

CHAPTER 3 *The Allure of the Mediterranean: Foundations of the Mediterranean Diet 29*

CHAPTER 4 *Building Your Meal Plan: Crafting Your Keto-Mediterranean Menu 43*

CHAPTER 5 *Recipes and Cooking Tips: Keto-Mediterranean Cuisine, Breakfast. 55*

CHAPTER 6 *Lunch Recipes 81*

CHAPTER 7 *Dinner Recipes 111*

CHAPTER 8 *Dessert Recipes 145*

CHAPTER 9: *Facing Challenges: How to Handle Common Obstacles and Initial Symptoms 179*

CHAPTER 10 *Physical Exercise and Keto-Mediterranean Diet: How to Optimize Results 191*

CHAPTER 11 *Long-Term Benefits: Heart Health, Weight Loss, and Beyond 203*

CHAPTER 12 *The Keto-Mediterranean Diet and Mental Health: The Mind-Body Connection 211*

CHAPTER 13 *Sustainability and Adaptability: Making the Keto-Mediterranean Diet a Lifestyle 221*

Here's a gift for YOU. 230

Copyright ©2023 by Mia Breeze.

All rights reserved. No part of this book may be reproduced, or stored in a retrieval system or transmitted in any form or by any means, electronic, mechanical, photocopying, recording, or otherwise without express written permission of the author. The reproduction of this work is forbidden without written consent from the author.

This eBook and paperback are licensed for your personal enjoyment only. This eBook and paperback may not be re-sold or given away to other people. If you would like to share this book with another person, please purchase an additional copy for each reader. If you're reading this book and did not purchase it, or it was not purchased for your use only, then please return and purchase your own copy. Thank you for respecting the hard work of this author.

Preface

Welcome to an adventure that will revolutionize how you think about food, health, and well-being. You hold in your hands not just a book, but a powerful key that unlocks the door to a new level of vitality, energy, and happiness. Imagine combining the fat-burning power of the ketogenic diet with the nutrient-rich flavors of the **Mediterranean diet**. Sounds like a dream. But I assure you, it's a reality. A reality that will introduce you to new tastes, effectively and sustainably shed weight, improve your heart health, and, not least, prolong your life.

But this isn't just a diet book. It's an invitation to embark on a **personal transformation journey**. It's a manual to understand how the food we eat can influence not only our bodies but our minds as well.

We will guide you step by step through every phase of your journey. You'll learn how to craft your personalized nutrition plan, overcome common challenges, and savor the delicious flavors of the **Keto-Mediterranean Diet**.

Are you ready to join us on this extraordinary journey towards a new way of living? Are you ready to feel more energetic, healthier, and happier than ever before? Then open this book and start your journey towards a better life. You are one step away from changing your life. **Are you ready?**

CHAPTER 1 Introduction to the Keto-Mediterranean Diet: The Best of Both Worlds

The ketogenic diet, or "keto" as it is commonly known, has its roots in medical studies dating back to the early 20th century. Initially, it was used to treat epilepsy in children, as it was discovered that a body in ketosis - a state in which the body burns fat for energy instead of carbohydrates - reduced the frequency of epileptic seizures. But it wasn't long before the ketogenic diet made its mark in the world of weight loss and fitness. The fundamental principle of the keto diet is a deficient intake of carbohydrates, paired with a high intake of fats and a suitable protein intake. This mix of macronutrients pushes the body into a state of ketosis, where it becomes an efficient fat-burning machine.

On the other hand, the Mediterranean diet, a pure reflection of the food traditions of the populations living around the Mediterranean Sea, has been celebrated for decades as one of the healthiest diets in the world. Rich in fresh fruits and vegetables, whole grains, legumes, fish, and olive oil, the Mediterranean diet is known for its protective properties against cardiovascular diseases and for promoting longevity.

Its emphasis on fresh and minimally processed ingredients offers a full range of essential nutrients, while the presence of healthy fats helps maintain a feeling of fullness.

At first glance, these two diets might seem opposites, with the ketogenic diet severely limiting carbohydrates and the Mediterranean diet celebrating them. However, the beauty of the Keto-Mediterranean Diet lies in this apparent contradiction.

The Keto-Mediterranean Diet combines the fat-burning efficiency of the ketogenic diet with the nutritional richness and variety of the Mediterranean diet. It allows you to harness the power of ketosis while maintaining a broader range of foods on your table. This blend not only allows for effective and sustainable weight loss but also promotes optimal heart health, improved cognitive function, and an overall sense of well-being.

We are about to embark on a journey of discovery through a food landscape that combines science and tradition, efficacy and pleasure, health, and taste. Welcome to the world of the Keto-Mediterranean Diet.

To successfully navigate the world of the Keto-Mediterranean Diet, it is essential to understand the key principles underlying both diets.

The Ketogenic Diet

The cornerstone of the ketogenic diet is the induction of a metabolic state called ketosis. Typically, your body uses carbohydrates as its primary energy source. However, when carbohydrate intake is drastically reduced, as in a ketogenic diet, your body is forced to seek an alternate energy source. It begins converting fats, both those you consume through the diet and those stored in your body, into ketone bodies, which are then used as fuel. This process can lead to rapid weight loss, as the body taps into its fat reserves for energy.

The Mediterranean Diet

The heart of the Mediterranean diet lies in the variety and quality of foods. This diet emphasizes fresh fruits and vegetables, whole grains, legumes, fish, and seafood, olive oil, nuts, and seeds. It also encourages moderate consumption of dairy, eggs, and poultry, and limits the use of red meats and refined sugars. The Mediterranean diet not only provides a broad spectrum of essential nutrients but also promotes heart health due to an abundance of monounsaturated and polyunsaturated fatty acids. Additionally, its emphasis on food variety and the enjoyment of food makes it sustainable in the long run.

The Keto-Mediterranean Diet

The combination of these two dietary approaches in the Keto-Mediterranean Diet creates a unique and powerful nutritional regimen. The Keto-Mediterranean Diet takes the low-carb and high-fat approach of the ketogenic diet but incorporates the wholesome foods and principles of variety and quality from the Mediterranean diet. In practice, this means that fat sources in the Keto-Mediterranean Diet will predominantly be healthy oils, nuts, seeds, fatty fish, and high-quality dairy, rather than foods high in saturated fats.

Adopting the Keto-Mediterranean Diet means prioritizing fresh and natural ingredients, choosing healthy fats, and limiting carbohydrate intake, yet without sacrificing variety and the joy of food. It not only allows you to achieve a state of ketosis for effective weight loss but also supplies you with all the essential nutrients for optimal health.

We are ready for a journey that will not only lead us to a leaner body but also to a healthier and longer life. And the best part is, we won't have to give up the pleasure of food. We are ready for the Keto-Mediterranean Diet.

After examining the foundations of both diets, the question might naturally arise: why combine the ketogenic and Mediterranean diets?

The answer lies in the potential of each diet and how their strengths can be harnessed to create a dietary regimen that maximizes health benefits.

Boosting Weight Loss

The ketogenic diet, with its focus on inducing ketosis, is a potent tool for weight loss. By dramatically reducing carbohydrate intake, the body is forced to burn fats for energy. This process can lead to significant weight loss, especially in the early stages of the diet.

However, a traditional keto diet can be monotonous and challenging to maintain in the long run. This is where the Mediterranean diet comes in. With its variety of foods and emphasis on fresh and flavorful ingredients, the Mediterranean diet can make the ketogenic approach more enjoyable and sustainable.

Promoting Heart Health

Another significant advantage of the Keto-Mediterranean Diet is its potential for heart health. The Mediterranean diet is renowned for its cardiovascular benefits, owing to its abundance of monounsaturated and polyunsaturated fats, antioxidants, and fiber.

By integrating these healthful principles with the ketogenic diet, the Keto-Mediterranean Diet can provide a pathway to weight loss that also supports heart health.

Foods such as olive oil, fatty fish, nuts, and seeds, all staple components of the Mediterranean diet, become primary fat sources in the Keto-Mediterranean Diet.

Supporting Brain Health

Lastly, combining the ketogenic and Mediterranean diets can have significant benefits for brain health. The ketogenic diet was originally developed to treat epilepsy, and recent studies suggest it may have positive effects on neurological conditions and overall brain health.

The Mediterranean diet, with its wide assortment of antioxidants, healthy fats, and nutrient-rich foods, has also been linked to a reduced risk of cognitive decline and neurodegenerative diseases. Incorporating elements from both diets into a single eating plan can thus support brain health alongside weight loss.

Merging the ketogenic diet with the Mediterranean diet in the Keto-Mediterranean Diet offers an innovative approach to nutrition. Not only does it provide a potent tool for weight loss, but it also promotes optimal health, supporting the heart, brain, and overall well-being. With the Keto-Mediterranean Diet, you can achieve your weight loss goals without sacrificing health or the joy of food.

There are countless diets, each with its unique strengths. However, when it comes to combining weight loss with overall well-being and long-term sustainability, the Keto-Mediterranean Diet may offer significant advantages over other dietary approaches. Let's see how it compares to some popular diets.

Keto-Mediterranean Diet vs Paleo

Diet The Paleo diet is based on the idea of eating like our Paleolithic ancestors, avoiding products of modern agriculture such as grains, dairy, and refined sugars. While the Paleo Diet can lead to weight loss and health improvements, it tends to be restrictive and can be difficult to follow in the long term. In contrast, the Keto-Mediterranean Diet, while maintaining a low-carb approach, emphasizes the quality and variety of foods, making it more flexible and sustainable. Moreover, the incorporation of high-quality dairy and legumes, avoided in the Paleo Diet, can provide additional health benefits.

Keto-Mediterranean Diet vs Vegan Diet

The vegan diet, which eliminates all animal products, is valued for its health and environmental benefits. However, it can be challenging to follow and requires careful planning to ensure an adequate intake of all essential nutrients.

The Keto-Mediterranean Diet, while being based on plant-based foods, also allows the consumption of fish, poultry, and dairy, making it easier to meet nutritional needs. Furthermore, the emphasis on food quality and sustainability aligns with many of the motivations behind the vegan diet.

Keto-Mediterranean Diet vs. Low-Fat Diet

Low-fat diets have long been recommended for weight loss and heart health. However, recent research has questioned the efficacy of a low-fat approach, suggesting that the quality of fats consumed might be more important than the total amount. The Keto-Mediterranean Diet emphasizes this very principle, encouraging the intake of healthy fats like those found in olive oil, fish, and nuts. Moreover, inducing ketosis might make the Keto-Mediterranean Diet more effective for weight loss compared to a low-fat diet. While each diet has its merits, the Keto-Mediterranean Diet stands out for its ability to combine the health benefits of two well-studied dietary approaches. It offers a path to weight loss that also emphasizes heart health, brain health, and food enjoyment, making it a unique and potent option within nutrition. The Keto-Mediterranean Diet, with its unique blend of nutritional and culinary principles, can offer a range of health and wellness benefits.

However, it's crucial to set realistic expectations when adopting this dietary lifestyle. Here's what you can expect.

Weight Loss

One of the main goals for many people embarking on the Keto-Mediterranean Diet is weight loss. Research has shown that both the ketogenic and Mediterranean diets can promote weight loss, and combining the two might amplify these effects. However, it's important to note that weight loss varies from individual to individual and depends on various factors, including diet adherence, physical activity level, and genetics. Nonetheless, the Keto-Mediterranean Diet provides a solid framework to promote weight loss through optimal and sustainable nutrition.

Improved Overall Health In addition to weight loss, the Keto-Mediterranean Diet can lead to improved overall health. This can include a reduced risk of heart disease, better blood sugar control, and improved brain health. Specifically, the Mediterranean diet has been linked to a lower risk of heart disease, owing to its rich content of healthy fats, fiber, and antioxidants. Likewise, the ketogenic diet has been shown to improve blood sugar control, which can be beneficial for individuals with insulin resistance or type 2 diabetes.

Longevity

The Keto-Mediterranean Diet may also support longevity.

The Mediterranean diet has been linked to longer life and a reduced risk of chronic diseases. While research on the ketogenic diet and longevity is still in its early stages, some studies suggest it might have anti-aging effects.

This diet can be a powerful tool for weight loss, overall health, and longevity. However, as with any lifestyle change, it's essential to set realistic expectations and take a balanced approach. Remember, the journey to optimal health is a journey, not a destination, and the Keto-Mediterranean Diet can be a valuable travel companion along this path.

CHAPTER 2 Understanding Ketosis: The Dietary Engine of the Ketogenic Diet

Ketosis is a natural metabolic process that occurs in your body when glucose (sugar) stores are low. During this state, the liver starts producing **ketones**, small fuel molecules, from **fats**, which the body uses as an alternative to glucose. Entering ketosis is the primary goal of the ketogenic diet and the dietary engine behind the Keto-Mediterranean Diet.

But what exactly does this mean from a biochemical perspective? Usually, your body uses **carbohydrates** as its main energy source. Carbohydrates are broken down into glucose, which is then utilized by the body's cells to produce energy. However, if carbohydrate intake is limited, as in the ketogenic diet, the body must resort to another energy source: **fats**. This is where ketosis comes into play. When the body is devoid of glucose, the liver starts breaking down fats, both from those you consume and those stored in your body, into fatty acids and glycerol. The fatty acids can further be broken down into **ketones**, which the body can use as an energy source.

Thus, ketosis is a state where the body is efficiently equipped to burn fats for energy, rather than relying on carbohydrates.

This makes the ketogenic diet, and consequently the Keto-Mediterranean Diet, an appealing option for those looking to lose weight or improve their metabolic health. Important to note, however, is that diet-induced ketosis is not the same as ketoacidosis, a potentially lethal condition that can occur in individuals with type 1 diabetes. While ketosis is a controlled process that produces a concentration of ketones in the blood sufficient to provide energy to the brain, ketoacidosis leads to dangerously high levels of ketones and sugars in the blood.

Understanding ketosis and how it functions is crucial to maximizing the benefits of the Keto-Mediterranean Diet. In the normal energy-producing process, the human body prioritizes using **carbohydrates**. When we consume foods rich in carbohydrates, they are broken down in our digestive system into simpler sugars, mainly glucose, which is then absorbed into the bloodstream. This glucose can either be used immediately to produce energy or can be stored in the liver and muscles as glycogen for future use.

This process is called **glycolysis**.

Glycolysis is the default metabolic pathway for most people.

However, when carbohydrate intake is insufficient, such as during fasting or when following a ketogenic diet, the body must find another energy source. This is when **ketosis** comes into play.

In ketosis, the body starts breaking down stored and dietary fats into molecules called **ketones**. These ketones serve as an alternative fuel when the glucose supply is low. It's important to note that ketosis is not an "abnormal" or harmful state for the body; it's simply an alternative way for the body to obtain energy. In fact, ketosis can be a sign that your body is burning fats efficiently.

The fundamental difference between glycolysis and ketosis concerns the energy source used by the body. In glycolysis, energy comes from the breakdown of carbohydrates, whereas in ketosis, energy comes from the breakdown of **fats**.

Transitioning from a state of glycolysis to ketosis can take some time, as the body needs to deplete glycogen stores and start producing and using ketones. This phase, often referred to as "keto flu", can be accompanied by some transient symptoms like fatigue, headaches, and irritability, but once the body adapts, many individuals report feeling more energetic and focused.

Understanding the distinction between glycolysis and ketosis is essential to grasp how the Keto-Mediterranean Diet works and how your body will adapt to this new dietary pattern. By following this diet, you will steer your body to become an efficient fat-burning machine, leveraging the benefits of ketosis to achieve your health and wellness goals.

If you now understand what entering ketosis means and the difference between glycolysis and ketosis, the next natural question would be, "How can I guide my body into ketosis?"

Inducing ketosis is primarily through diet, although physical exercise and intermittent fasting can accelerate the process.

In the Keto-Mediterranean Diet, the goal is to limit carbohydrate intake and increase the consumption of healthy fats. Below, we'll explore some key strategies to induce ketosis through diet:

Limit carbohydrate intake: This is the most crucial step. To induce ketosis, you need to limit your carbohydrate intake to 20-50 grams a day.

This forces your body to seek another energy source, initiating the ketosis process.

Increase intake of healthy fats: To replace carbohydrates in your diet, you'll increase your intake of healthy fats. Foods rich in monounsaturated and polyunsaturated fats, such as olive oil, fatty fish, nuts, and seeds, should become a central part of your diet.

Moderate protein intake: While it's essential to consume protein to maintain muscle mass during a ketogenic regimen, an excess of protein can hinder ketosis. This is because excess protein can be converted to glucose in the body, interfering with ketosis.

Hydration: Drink plenty of water. Ketosis can lead to the loss of electrolytes, and water helps replenish them.

Physical activity: Even though physical activity is not strictly related to diet; it can help speed up the ketosis process. Exercise helps deplete glycogen in the body, making it switch to ketosis more quickly. Inducing ketosis can take time and may require some adjustments. It's essential to listen to your body and make changes based on your individual needs.

Monitoring ketosis levels is a critical aspect of maintaining the success of the Keto-Mediterranean Diet.

Knowing if your body is in ketosis helps you determine if you're correctly following the diet and gives you the chance to make changes if necessary.

There are several techniques you can use to monitor ketosis:

Urine test: Urine tests for ketosis are widely available and can be a simple, non-invasive way to determine if your body is in ketosis. These tests detect the presence of ketones in the urine.

However, they are less accurate than blood tests, and their effectiveness may diminish over time as your body adjusts to ketosis and becomes more efficient at using ketones.

Blood test: Blood tests for ketones are the most accurate. They measure the level of a particular ketone, beta-hydroxybutyrate, in your blood. This is the primary ketone your body produces when in ketosis. Although blood tests are more accurate, they are also more expensive and require a small blood sample.

Breath test: These tests measure the amount of acetone, a type of ketone, in your breath. Acetone is a byproduct of ketosis and is expelled from the body through the breath. Breath tests aren't as accurate as blood tests but are more convenient than urine tests.

Besides these monitoring tools, there are some physical signals that can indicate you're in ketosis. These include weight loss, reduced appetite, increased energy and focus, fruity-smelling breath (due to acetone), and, in some cases, dry mouth or frequent thirst. Remember, however, that these are just general indications and can vary from person to person.

Monitoring ketosis allows you to stay focused on your journey and helps you understand how the Keto-Mediterranean Diet affects your body.

With the right knowledge and tools, you're in a strong position to maximize the benefits of ketosis.

Despite the numerous advantages that ketosis can offer, it's essential to be aware of possible side effects that can manifest, especially during the early stages of adapting to the Keto-Mediterranean Diet. These symptoms, often known as "keto flu," can include fatigue, headaches, dizziness, irritability, constipation, and sleep issues.

Here's how to tackle some of these common symptoms:

Fatigue and weakness: During the early stages of the diet, your body is still learning to switch from using glucose as its primary energy source to using ketones. This change can lead to fatigue. Ensure you get adequate rest and allow yourself the time to adjust.

A good intake of minerals can also help, as the loss of electrolytes can contribute to this sense of fatigue.

Headaches: This symptom often arises from dehydration or the loss of electrolytes. Increasing water intake and ensuring an adequate intake of minerals can help prevent or alleviate headaches.

Dizziness: Like headaches, dizziness can be caused by dehydration and electrolyte loss. Maintaining good hydration levels and an adequate intake of minerals can help prevent this symptom.

Constipation: Switching to a high-fat, low-carb diet can result in a decrease in fiber intake, which can cause constipation. Make sure to include fiber-rich foods in your diet, such as leafy green vegetables and seeds.

Irritability and sleep problems: These symptoms are common during the adaptation phase when the body is learning to use ketones as its primary energy source. These symptoms tend to diminish once your body has adapted to the new energy source. Remember, ketosis is a natural metabolic state, and, with proper preparation and management, its side effects can be effectively managed. If side effects persist or become severe, it is always advisable to consult a health professional. Ketosis can be a powerful ally in your weight loss journey.

But how exactly does it work? How does it promote fat loss, and how can it help keep appetite in check?

Firstly, it's useful to remember that ketosis occurs when the body depletes its glucose reserves and begins to use ketones as its main energy source. This process forces the body to use fat reserves for energy, thus contributing to weight loss. Additionally, being in a state of ketosis can help control appetite. When the body uses ketones for energy, it tends to feel full for a longer period. This is because ketones can reduce levels of ghrelin, the hunger hormone, and increase levels of cholecystokinin (CCK), a hormone that promotes satiety.

This combination can help reduce appetite and prevent overeating. Ketosis can also boost metabolism. When the body is in a state of ketosis, it burns fat at a higher rate. This increased metabolic rate can help burn more calories, further promoting weight loss. It's important to note that ketosis is just one tool in the weight loss journey. It's not a magic solution, and weight loss still requires concerted effort and a balanced approach to diet and exercise. This is where the combination of the ketogenic diet with the dietary pattern of the Mediterranean diet comes into play. The Keto-Mediterranean Diet combines the benefits of ketosis with the balanced and sustainable approach of the Mediterranean diet.

This combination offers a healthy and sustainable eating plan that can promote weight loss, improve overall health, and promote a sense of well-being. With this, we've concluded our exploration of ketosis and its role in the Keto-Mediterranean Diet. In the next chapter, we'll delve into the heart of the Mediterranean, exploring the foundations of the Mediterranean Diet and how we can integrate it with ketogenic principles to create an optimal dietary approach.

CHAPTER 3 The Allure of the Mediterranean: Foundations of the Mediterranean Diet

Many diets come and go, but the Mediterranean Diet has stood the test of time. Rooted in centuries of tradition and culture, this diet has become famous not just for its health benefits, but also for its deep connection to a unique and sustainable way of life.

The roots of the Mediterranean Diet trace back to the times of ancient Greece and Rome, where food was seen not just as nourishment, but also as a pleasure to be shared with family and friends. Even back then, the main components of the diet were fruits, vegetables, whole grains, legumes, fish, wine, and olive oil—all local products that reflected the abundance of the Mediterranean lands.

Over the centuries, the Mediterranean Diet absorbed influences from various cultures that settled around the Mediterranean basin, enriching itself with new flavors and culinary traditions.

Be it the couscous from North Africa, the Greek tzatziki, the Spanish gazpacho, or the Italian risotto, the

Mediterranean Diet is a veritable melting pot of tastes and cultures.

However, the Mediterranean Diet only gained global acclaim in the 20th century when scientists began studying the dietary patterns of Mediterranean populations. They were particularly struck by the low rates of heart disease and the longevity of residents in Crete and southern Italy, despite post-war economic hardships.

These observations led to the birth of the concept of the "Mediterranean Diet", a dietary model that seemed to safeguard health despite inadequate healthcare. Today, the Mediterranean Diet is deemed one of the healthiest and most sustainable dietary models in the world, recognized by UNESCO as an Intangible Cultural Heritage of Humanity.

As we delve deeper into the Mediterranean Diet in this chapter, remember that we are not just discussing a set of dietary guidelines. We are exploring an approach to food and life that has been shaped by centuries of history and continues to impact the health and well-being of millions worldwide.

The Mediterranean Diet is a mosaic of nutrient-rich ingredients, intense flavors, and authentic culinary traditions.

It's a dietary model that favors natural, minimally processed, and seasonal foods, centered around a few fundamental nutritional pillars.

Fruits and Vegetables: These colorful foods are the backbone of the Mediterranean Diet.

Rich in vitamins, minerals, fiber, and phytochemicals, fruits and vegetables help meet daily nutrient requirements and protect the body from diseases like obesity, diabetes, and heart disease. Whether it's sun-ripened tomatoes from Italy, juicy oranges from Spain, Greek eggplants, or sweet dates from North Africa, fruits and vegetables offer a rainbow of flavors and nutrients that are good for both the palate and health.

Whole Grains and Legumes: These sources of complex carbohydrates are valuable for their intake of fiber, plant-based proteins, B vitamins, and minerals. Be it spelt, barley, couscous, lentils, chickpeas, or beans, whole grains, and legumes take center stage in many Mediterranean recipes, helping to promote feelings of fullness and regulate blood sugar.

Fish and Seafood: The Mediterranean is known for its variety of fish and seafood, which are an excellent source of lean proteins and omega-3 fatty acids, beneficial for heart and brain health.

Sardines, anchovies, seabass, bream, squid, shrimp, and octopus are just a few examples of what the Mediterranean offers.

Olive Oil: This "liquid gold" is the primary fat used in the Mediterranean Diet.

Rich in monounsaturated fats and antioxidants, extra virgin olive oil is celebrated for its protective effects on the heart and arteries.

It's generously used in salads, for cooking, and even as a bread dip.

Wine: A glass of wine, especially red, is often found on the Mediterranean table, consumed in moderation and usually with meals. Polyphenols in red wine, like resveratrol, have shown potential heart health benefits.

These foods not only make up a nourishing diet but also provide a rich and satisfying culinary experience. The Mediterranean Diet is a celebration of food in its most natural and delicious state, a sensory journey that delights the palate and nourishes the body.

When talking about the Mediterranean Diet, one cannot fail to mention the numerous health benefits this dietary model offers. Countless scientific studies have hailed it as one of the healthiest diets in the world, capable of preventing and managing a variety of health conditions.

Prevention of Cardiovascular Diseases: The heart and arteries benefit greatly from the Mediterranean Diet. Its foods, rich in monounsaturated fats, fibers, antioxidants, and omega-3s, work synergistically to reduce LDL cholesterol (the so-called "bad cholesterol"), lower blood pressure, reduce inflammation, and improve the function of blood vessels.

This helps decrease the risk of cardiovascular diseases like hypertension, atherosclerosis, and heart attacks.

Weight Management and Obesity Prevention: The Mediterranean Diet features a low content of refined sugars and saturated fats and a high intake of fibers and proteins. This balance promotes satiety, helps prevent glycemic fluctuations, and encourages sustainable weight loss over time.

Protection from Diabetes: Low glycemic index foods, fibers, and healthy fats are pillars that make the Mediterranean Diet an excellent tool for preventing and managing type 2 diabetes. These elements help maintain stable blood sugar levels and improve insulin sensitivity.

Longevity and Overall Well-being: Mediterranean populations are renowned for their longevity and low rates of chronic diseases. Many attribute this longevity to diet, which supplies a wide variety of essential nutrients, keeps the body healthy, and promotes overall well-being.

The importance of the Mediterranean Diet in disease prevention cannot be understated. It's a powerful shield against the most common afflictions of our time, ensuring health delivered on a plate in a symphony of flavors, colors, and aromas that make food a pleasure, not a penance. It not only prevents diseases but also promotes a long, quality life.

The soul of the Mediterranean Diet resides in its food pyramid, visually representing the proportions of various foods to consume for a balanced and healthy diet.

At the pyramid's base, we find foods to be consumed daily and in greater amounts. Here we find whole grains like rice, pasta, bread, barley, and couscous, rich in fibers, vitamins, and minerals. These foods should constitute the bulk of the daily caloric intake.

The pyramid's second level is reserved for fruits, vegetables, and legumes, also to be consumed daily. They provide fibers, vitamins, minerals, and antioxidants, essential for maintaining health and disease prevention.

The third level includes dairy, nuts, eggs, and fish. These should be consumed in moderate amounts, on average every two days. They provide high-quality proteins, omega-3 fatty acids, vitamins, and minerals.

Finally, atop the pyramid, we find high-fat and high-sugar foods, like sweets and red meats. These should be consumed in moderation, preferably just once a week or on special occasions.

The Mediterranean food pyramid is a flexible and adaptable model, meeting the nutritional needs of different age groups, genders, and lifestyles. Alongside following the pyramid, it's crucial to maintain an active lifestyle, drink plenty of water, and limit salt intake.

Moreover, a fundamental aspect of the Mediterranean model is the focus on food quality and origin. Fresh, local, and seasonal ingredients are favored over processed and industrial ones. Food preparation also plays a significant role; cooking techniques should preserve nutrients and natural flavors as much as possible.

The Mediterranean Diet's allure isn't just in food choice. This diet celebrates food as a joy source, encouraging meal sharing with friends and family. And it's a salute to health and longevity, a nutritional and cultural heritage to safeguard and promote.

The Mediterranean Diet is more than just a dietary regimen; it embodies a holistic well-being view. This lifestyle mirrors the life philosophy of Mediterranean basin populations, marked by harmony between humans and nature, community importance, and a slower, more mindful life pace.

First and foremost, regular physical activity is a cornerstone of the Mediterranean lifestyle. This doesn't necessarily mean intense gym workouts but incorporates general daily physical activity. This might include daily walks, gardening, swimming, or cycling. Every movement count, contributing to an individual's overall well-being.

Secondly, the Mediterranean Diet emphasizes the importance of community and socialization. Meals are often enjoyed in the company of family and friends, turning every meal into an occasion for sharing and communion. This strengthens social ties and offers significant psychological benefits, reducing stress and increasing feelings of belonging and happiness.

Moderate wine consumption, especially red wine, is another characteristic feature of the Mediterranean lifestyle. Red wine is rich in polyphenols, and antioxidants that have been shown to have beneficial effects on the cardiovascular system.

However, it is essential to remember that wine should be consumed in moderation, preferably during meals, to avoid the negative effects of alcohol abuse.

Finally, the Mediterranean lifestyle encourages a positive and relaxed attitude towards life. In the hectic chaos of the modern world, the Mediterranean philosophy invites us to slow down, take time for ourselves, savor every bite, and enjoy the beauty of nature that surrounds us.

By adopting the Mediterranean lifestyle, you are not only choosing a way to feed yourself but also a way to live. You are choosing to nourish not just your body, but also your mind and spirit.

And in this choice lies the true charm of the Mediterranean, a promise of well-being and longevity that goes beyond a simple plate of pasta.

Incorporating the essence of the Mediterranean Diet into our daily lives is not just about what we eat, but also how and when we eat it. Changing eating habits isn't always easy, but familiarizing ourselves with typical recipes and Mediterranean eating customs can facilitate this journey.

The Mediterranean Diet revolves around the main meals: breakfast, lunch, and dinner, enriched by small snacks.

Breakfast is often light, consisting of a whole grain option like bread or oatmeal, along with fresh fruit and a protein source like cheese or yogurt. A classic example is a bowl of Greek yogurt with honey and walnuts, accompanied by a slice of whole grain bread.

For lunch and dinner, the emphasis is on fresh vegetables, legumes, whole grains, and lean proteins. A lunch example could be a lentil soup accompanied by a fresh salad and whole grain bread. For dinner, one might opt for a baked fish dish with a side of grilled vegetables and a serving of bulgur or quinoa.

The key is to vary as much as possible, using a wide range of foods to achieve a balanced and nutritionally dense diet.

Snacks are useful to maintain stable blood sugar levels between main meals. Healthy snack options include fresh fruit, nuts and seeds, yogurt, or raw vegetables with hummus.

In terms of eating habits, the Mediterranean approach emphasizes the importance of eating slowly and mindfully. This means taking the time to savor each bite and listening to the body's satiety signals. This practice not only improves digestion but also contributes to a sense of fullness and satisfaction, helping to prevent overconsumption.

Moreover, the Mediterranean Diet promotes the idea of eating in company. Sharing meals with family and friends not only makes the eating experience more enjoyable but can also help moderate portions and maintain a healthy relationship with food.

We have delved into the details of the Mediterranean Diet, celebrating its flavorful dishes, its rich mosaic of healthy ingredients, and its rituals of conviviality. But how can we combine this experience with the Ketogenic Diet without compromising ketosis?

The answer lies in wisely balancing foods. While the Mediterranean Diet embraces a wide range of foods, we need to select those that best align with ketogenic requirements.

For instance, one should prioritize the intake of healthy fats such as olive oil, fatty fish, nuts, and seeds, being careful to limit carbohydrate intake.

Leafy green vegetables, tomatoes, peppers, cucumbers, and zucchinis are all excellent for the keto diet and are staple ingredients of Mediterranean cuisine. These can be consumed abundantly, providing essential nutrients without burdening the carbohydrate load.

Proteins should primarily come from lean sources like fish and chicken meat, limiting red meats to occasional consumption. Even though the Mediterranean Diet includes moderate intake of whole grains and legumes, these should be consumed cautiously in a Keto-Mediterranean Diet, given their high carbohydrate content.

Fruit, another pillar of the Mediterranean Diet, can be incorporated with caution. Fruits like berries can be consumed in small amounts due to their relatively low carbohydrate content and their high nutrient density.

The social side of eating is another aspect to consider. The Mediterranean Diet encourages communal meals and the sharing of dishes, a habit that can easily be carried into the Keto-Mediterranean Diet. Sharing meals not only creates a supportive environment but also makes food more enjoyable and fulfilling.

Combining these two dietary worlds is not only possible, but it can lead to a healthier and more satisfying life. The Keto-Mediterranean Diet offers a balance between effective and sustainable weight loss and the enjoyment of tasty and nutritious foods.

We therefore conclude this chapter with the certainty that the Keto-Mediterranean Diet is not just an intriguing idea, but a fully achievable reality. We hope that you, the reader, feel motivated to embrace this lifestyle, experiencing the advantages of two incredible worlds combined. Remember, the journey is as important as the destination. In the following pages, we will continue to explore the path to a healthier and more vibrant future through the Keto-Mediterranean Diet. Keep reading, the journey has just begun.

CHAPTER 4 Building Your Meal Plan: Crafting Your Keto-Mediterranean Menu

Starting with a well-defined goal is essential for any journey, and the quest for a healthier life with the Keto-Mediterranean Diet is no exception. A clear goal will give you the motivation to make the right food choices every day, keep you on track during challenging times, and ultimately help you see and appreciate the progress you're making.

Whether you're looking to lose weight, gain muscle mass, improve your overall health, or achieve a mix of these goals, the Keto-Mediterranean Diet can be your ally. This unique diet offers the benefits of both diets - the weight loss and metabolic advantages of the ketogenic diet, and the longevity and cardiovascular health of the Mediterranean diet.

To set your goals, start by thinking about where you are now and where you want to be. Consider not just your weight or physical appearance but also your overall health. Think about how you feel, your energy levels, your sleep, your mood. All these factors can be influenced by your diet.

Next, set specific, measurable, achievable, realistic, and time-bound goals - the SMART goals. For example, instead of saying "I want to lose weight," try saying "I want to lose 5 kg in the next 3 months." Having a specific goal will help you stay focused and give you a sense of direction.

Remember, it's essential to be kind to yourself during this process. Every individual is unique, and so is their journey towards a healthier life. There can be ups and downs, and that's okay. What matters is taking one step at a time toward your goal.

Calculating your daily macronutrients is the fundamental pillar to tailor the Keto-Mediterranean Diet to your specific needs. By "macros," we mean proteins, fats, and carbohydrates, the three main types of nutrients we get from food. Calculating macros is an essential tool to reach your goals, whether you wish to lose weight, gain muscle mass, or simply maintain an optimal nutritional balance.

Let's start with the key to the Keto-Mediterranean Diet: fats. Contrary to common belief, fats are not the enemy. In the keto diet, fats are the primary energy source. Therefore, about 70% of your daily calories should come from fats.

Most of these should be from unsaturated fats, favoring foods like olive oil, fatty fish, nuts, and seeds.

Proteins are the second macro to consider. They are crucial for tissue repair and growth, including muscles. For the Keto-Mediterranean Diet, protein should account for about 20-25% of daily calories. Protein-rich foods like fish, eggs, poultry, and some cheese varieties are excellent choices.

Lastly, there are the carbohydrates. In the keto diet, carbohydrates are significantly reduced compared to a standard diet. This prompts your body to enter ketosis, a state where it burns fat for energy instead of carbohydrates. For the Keto-Mediterranean Diet, carbohydrates should only make up about 5-10% of daily calories.

And remember, quality counts. Choose complex carbs such as those from leafy greens, broccoli, zucchini, and so forth.

It's important to note that these percentages are general guidelines. Every individual is unique and may need to adjust these percentages based on their specific needs. Calculating macros is not an exact science and might require some trial and error. Over time, you will better understand how your body responds to different amounts of macros and can adjust your diet accordingly.

The goal is to create a sustainable meal plan that helps you achieve your long-term health goals.

To progress on your journey towards health and wellness with the Keto-Mediterranean Diet, it's essential to know and carefully choose the foods that will aid in reaching your goals. This selection is based on nutritional quality, energy density, and the ability to satisfy appetite while keeping the body in a state of ketosis.

Let's first talk about fats, the predominant nutrient in the keto diet. High-quality fats are crucial and should mainly come from sources of unsaturated fats.

These include extra virgin olive oil, fatty fish like salmon, nuts and seeds, and avocados. Besides being rich in healthy fats, these foods also provide a variety of other essential nutrients.

Regarding proteins, the best choices are those high in protein but low in carbohydrates. Chicken, turkey, fish, and eggs are excellent choices. Cheese, especially low-carb ones like feta and mozzarella, can be consumed in moderation.

When it comes to carbohydrates, the key is to choose low-carb, high-fiber foods. Leafy greens like spinach and kale, as well as other non-starchy vegetables like bell peppers, broccoli, and zucchini, are all excellent choices.

For fruits, prioritize those low in sugar like berries and forest fruits.

Remember to avoid refined sugars, refined grains, and other high-carb foods.

Not only will they prevent you from entering ketosis, but they also don't offer much nutritional value.

Choosing foods is not just about nutrition but also personal tastes. The beauty of the Keto-Mediterranean Diet lies in its flexibility.

Explore, experiment, and find that combination of foods that makes you feel full, energetic, and happy.

After all, you're not just following a diet; you're adopting a new, healthy, and sustainable lifestyle.

Organization is a key element for the success of the Keto-Mediterranean Diet. Careful meal and expense planning will not only save you time and money but will also make your transition to this lifestyle smoother and stress-free. Here are some helpful tips for efficient planning.

Plan your meals. First and foremost, it's important to create a meal plan for the week. Consider your goals, lifestyle, and preferences. Try to vary your meals to avoid monotony and ensure a wide variety of nutrients. Remember to balance the macros in every meal, including sources of protein, healthy fats, and a moderate amount of carbohydrates from low-carb vegetables.

Make a shopping list. After deciding on your meals, create a shopping list. This will help you avoid impulsive purchases and focus on what's truly necessary.

Aim to buy mainly fresh and minimally processed foods. Remember that the quality of food is as important as the quantity.

Save with bulk buying. If possible, buy staple foods in bulk, such as olive oil, meat, dairy products, and long-lasting vegetables. This will save you money and ensure you always have the basic ingredients for your Keto-Mediterranean dishes on hand.

Prepare meals in advance. Preparing meals ahead of time is another effective way to save time during the week. You can cook in larger quantities and then freeze portions for subsequent days. For instance, you could prepare a large batch of vegetable soup or cook several chicken breasts to use in different dishes.

Don't forget the snacks. Snacks are crucial for maintaining steady energy levels throughout the day. Think of snacks that are easy to prepare and take with you. Nuts, olives, low-carb cheeses, and seafood are all great options.

Don't be afraid to modify the plan. Flexibility is essential. If one day you don't feel like having the meal you planned or if an ingredient is unavailable, don't hesitate to make changes. Your plan should be a help, not a source of stress.

Meal and shopping planning is an investment in your well-being. It will help you stay on track, save time and money, and make your Keto-Mediterranean Diet a pleasant, stress-free experience.

The journey toward a new dietary lifestyle, like the Keto-Mediterranean Diet, requires commitment, patience, and attention. It's essential to monitor your progress and make necessary adjustments to ensure the diet is sustainable and rewarding. Here are some tools and strategies to support your journey.

Measure progress. The most direct way to monitor progress is to track your weight and body measurements. However, these aren't the only indicators of success. The Keto-Mediterranean Diet aims to improve not just your appearance but also your overall health and well-being.

So, also consider other indicators, such as energy levels, sleep quality, mood, mental clarity, and health parameters like blood pressure and blood sugar levels.

Keep a food diary. Recording what you eat daily can be a great tool to understand how food affects your body and well-being. This can help you identify foods that make you feel energetic and those that might cause fatigue or bloating. The food diary can also make you more aware of your eating habits and lead to more informed choices.

Adapt your meal plan. Everybody is unique and can react differently to the same foods. If you notice that a particular food or combination of foods doesn't make you feel good, or if you're not reaching your goals even though you're following the plan, you might need to make some adjustments. Don't hesitate to consult a nutritionist or doctor if you need personalized advice.

Stick to your "Why". Remembering the reason why you decided to follow the Keto-Mediterranean Diet can be a great motivator in challenging times. Whether you want to lose weight, improve your health, or just try a new way of eating, keeping in mind your "why" can help you stay motivated and focused on your goal.

Celebrate your successes. Every small step forward is a success. Don't wait to reach your goal to celebrate.

Acknowledge your efforts and celebrate your progress, no matter how small. This can boost your motivation and give you the push to continue your journey.

Monitoring your progress and making necessary adjustments will help you create a Keto-Mediterranean meal plan that perfectly suits your needs and lifestyle. The key to success is patience, consistency, and paying attention to your body. You are on the right path to a healthier and more satisfying life.

Creating delicious, nutritious dishes aligned with the Keto-Mediterranean Diet might seem challenging, but it's an opportunity to experiment in the kitchen and discover new flavor combinations. The secret is maintaining a balance between essential macronutrients while prioritizing wholesome, natural foods. To provide practical assistance, I'll share some tips and recipe ideas to inspire you to create your own Keto-Mediterranean dishes.

Start with the basics. Mediterranean dishes often rely on a set of key ingredients. Olive oil, garlic, onions, tomatoes, peppers, zucchini, eggplants, and a wide variety of herbs can form the foundation for countless dishes. For instance, ratatouille is an excellent vegetable-based side dish that can be easily adapted to the keto diet by removing or limiting high-carb ingredients.

Protein at the forefront. Lean meats, fish, and seafood are all excellent protein sources. A chicken salad with leafy greens, tomatoes, cucumbers, feta, and a generous drizzle of olive oil can be a complete meal. Another example might be grilled fish with a lemon and olive oil sauce, accompanied by grilled vegetables.

Play with fats. Don't be afraid to use healthy fats in your cooking. An avocado stuffed with tuna and homemade mayo or a vegetable soup enriched with cream or cheese are great keto meal options. Remember, fats will help you feel fuller for longer.

Experiment with spices. Spices not only add flavor to your dishes but also offer various health benefits. You can use basil, oregano, rosemary, thyme, and many other herbs to diversify the taste of your recipes.

Consider texture. Texture also plays a significant role in making a dish enjoyable. You can vary the texture of your dishes by using different cooking methods and combining ingredients of different consistencies.

Now, you're ready to put these tips into practice and craft your Keto-Mediterranean recipes. There's no "right" or "wrong" recipe. Everyone is unique, and what works for one might not work for another. So, experiment, personalize, and most importantly, enjoy your journey towards a healthier lifestyle.

Now that you've learned to create your own Keto-Mediterranean meal plan, you're ready to implement these principles with some delicious and nutritious recipes. In the next chapter, I'll guide you through a variety of Keto-Mediterranean dishes that not only meet your nutritional goals but will also delight your palate. We'll dive into the captivating world of Mediterranean flavors combined with the power of ketosis. Get ready to discover new ways of enjoying your favorite foods and experiment with tastes that will elevate your culinary experience to a whole new level. I can't wait to share these delightful recipes with you!

CHAPTER 5 Recipes and Cooking Tips: Keto-Mediterranean Cuisine, Breakfast.

1.Keto Pancakes with Berries and Cream

Start your day with something sweet without compromising your keto goals. These keto pancakes made with almond and coconut flour are the perfect breakfast to fill you up and give you energy for the whole morning. Topped with fresh berries and whipped cream for a final touch of sweetness.

Ingredients:

- 100g almond flour
- 50g coconut flour
- 2 eggs
- 200ml almond milk
- 1 teaspoon baking powder
- A pinch of salt
- Mixed fresh berries for garnish
- Whipped cream for garnish

Preparation:

1. In a bowl, combine the almond flour, coconut flour, baking powder, and salt.
2. In another bowl, whisk the eggs and add the almond milk.
3. Add your wet ingredients to your dry ingredients and mix until you get a smooth batter.
4. Heat a non-stick pan over medium heat and pour a ladle of batter. Cook each side of the pancake for 2-3 minutes or until golden.
5. Serve your pancakes with a handful of fresh berries and a dollop of whipped cream.

These keto pancakes with berries and cream represent a delicious and keto-friendly breakfast that won't make you miss traditional high-carb sweets. Experiment with different types of berries for variations in taste and presentation.

2. Keto Blueberry Muffins

Dive into the sweet and natural taste of blueberries with these keto muffins. Made with almond flour, they are the perfect way to satisfy your sweet cravings without exiting ketosis.

Ingredients:

- 200g almond flour
- 50g keto-friendly sweetener (erythritol or xylitol)
- 2 eggs
- 60g melted butter
- 100g fresh blueberries
- 1 teaspoon baking powder
- A pinch of salt

Preparation:

1. Preheat the oven to 180°C and prepare a muffin tin by lining with paper cups.
2. In a bowl, combine the almond flour, sweetener, baking powder, and salt.
3. In another bowl, whisk the eggs and add the melted butter.
4. Slowly add the dry ingredients to the wet, mixing until a smooth batter forms.
5. Gently fold in the blueberries.
6. Fill each muffin cup about 2/3 full, then bake for 15-20 minutes or until a toothpick inserted in the center comes out clean.
7. Let the muffins cool in the tin for 5 minutes, then transfer them to a rack to cool completely.

These keto blueberry muffins are a real treat for the palate and perfect for breakfast or an afternoon snack. Their sweet taste and nutritional intake make them an excellent choice for those following the keto-Mediterranean diet. Experiment with different keto-friendly sweeteners or add nuts or seeds for additional flavor and texture variations.

3.Keto Green Smoothie

Kickstart your day with a boost of vitality thanks to this keto green smoothie. Rich in vitamins and minerals, it's a refreshing mix of spinach, avocado, cucumber, and lemon, naturally sweetened for a perfect balance of flavor.

Ingredients:

- 1 cup fresh spinach
- 1 ripe avocado
- 1 small cucumber
- Juice of 1 lemon
- 1-2 teaspoons keto-friendly sweetener (like erythritol)
- 1 cup water or unsweetened almond milk

Preparation:

1. Wash the spinach, cucumber, and lemon thoroughly.
2. Peel the avocado and remove the pit.
3. Cut the cucumber into pieces.
4. Place the spinach, avocado, and cucumber in the blender.
5. Add the lemon juice and sweetener.
6. Pour the water or almond milk into the blender.
7. Blend until you get a smooth and creamy consistency.

This keto green smoothie is an explosion of nourishment in a glass. It's a perfect option for breakfast or an afternoon snack, providing a wealth of nutrients while remaining low in carbs. Remember, you can always customize your smoothie with different leafy greens or by adding chia seeds or protein powder for an extra protein boost.

4. Mediterranean Keto Frittata

Start your day with a delicious Mediterranean frittata, rich in protein and healthy fats. A perfect mix of eggs, fresh vegetables, feta cheese, and the final touch, olive oil.

Ingredients:

- 6 eggs
- 1 small onion
- 1 bell pepper
- 100g feta cheese
- 2 tablespoons olive oil
- Salt and pepper to taste

Preparation:

1. Whisk the eggs in a bowl and add salt and pepper.
2. In a non-stick pan, sauté the onion and bell pepper in olive oil until they soften.
3. Add the eggs and cook over medium heat. When the eggs start to set, add the crumbled feta cheese and cover the pan.
4. Cook for another 2-3 minutes or until the eggs are fully cooked.

This Mediterranean frittata is an example of how the keto-Mediterranean diet can be tasty and nutritious. Rich in protein and healthy fats, it will help you maintain ketosis without giving up Mediterranean flavors. We will follow this format for all recipes presented in the chapter. Remember, each recipe is a suggestion: feel free to customize them to your liking, always respecting the guidelines of the keto-Mediterranean diet.

5. Flaxseed Keto Porridge

The Flaxseed Keto Porridge is a delightful low-carb breakfast, perfect for those on a ketogenic diet. This gluten-free porridge is made from flaxseeds, which are rich in fiber and omega-3 fatty acids. With a creamy consistency and a slightly sweet taste, this porridge will provide you with sustained energy to start the day. Follow our recipe to prepare this simple and nutritious keto porridge.

Ingredients:

- 3 tablespoons of flaxseeds
- 1 cup of water or unsweetened almond milk
- 1 teaspoon of ground cinnamon
- 1 teaspoon of sweetener of choice (stevia, erythritol, xylitol)
- Fresh or dried fruit for garnish (optional)

Preparation:

1. Begin by grinding the flaxseeds in a coffee grinder or blender until they reach a flour-like consistency. This will help absorb water during cooking.

2. In a small pot, add the ground flaxseeds, water or almond milk, ground cinnamon, and your chosen sweetener. Mix well to combine.

3. Bring the mixture to a boil over medium-high heat, then reduce the heat to medium-low and continue cooking for about 5 minutes, stirring occasionally. The porridge will thicken as it cooks.

4. Once the desired consistency is reached, turn off the heat and let the porridge sit for a few minutes, allowing the flaxseeds to further absorb the moisture.

5. Transfer the flaxseed porridge to a bowl and garnish with your choice of fresh or dried fruit.

6. The Flaxseed Keto Porridge is ready to be enjoyed! Serve warm and savor this fiber-rich, nutrient-packed breakfast.

The Flaxseed Keto Porridge is a nourishing and tasty breakfast, ideal for those on a low-carb diet. Made from flaxseeds, this porridge delivers a wealth of fiber and omega-3 fatty acids, essential for good health. With a creamy consistency and a hint of sweetness, this porridge will provide a lasting energy boost to start your day. Choose your favorite fresh or dried fruit to garnish and tailor this dish to your liking. Prepare it following our recipe and enjoy a delicious and healthy breakfast that will sustain you until lunch.

6.Keto Waffles with Strawberries and Cream

For days when you want a special breakfast without deviating from your keto plan, these keto waffles with strawberries and cream are the perfect choice. Made with coconut and almond flour, they are delightfully crispy and light, and served with fresh strawberries and whipped cream for a touch of sweetness and creaminess.

Ingredients:

- 1 cup of almond flour
- 1/2 cup of coconut flour
- 2 teaspoons of baking powder
- 1 teaspoon of keto-friendly sweetener (such as erythritol)
- A pinch of salt
- 4 large eggs
- 1 cup of unsweetened almond milk
- Fresh strawberries for garnish
- Whipped cream for garnish

Preparation:

1. In a large bowl, mix together the almond flour, coconut flour, baking powder, sweetener, and salt.
2. In another bowl, beat the eggs and add the almond milk.
3. Slowly add the wet ingredients to the dry ones, stirring until they are fully combined.
4. Heat your waffle iron and pour in a portion of the batter. Cook until the waffles are golden and crispy.
5. Serve your waffles with fresh strawberries and whipped cream as desired.

The keto waffles with strawberries and cream are a real treat to start the day. Rich in protein and healthy fats, they are perfect to keep you energetic and full throughout the morning. Remember, the beauty of the keto diet is the ability to enjoy the food you love with some minor adjustments!

7.Poached Eggs on Sautéed Spinach

Poached Eggs on Sautéed Spinach is a simple yet flavorful dish, ideal for a healthy breakfast or a light lunch. The eggs, with their soft and runny yolk, are served on a bed of sautéed spinach, adding freshness and nutrients to the dish. Follow our step-by-step recipe to prepare this delicious and nutritious meal.

Ingredients:

- 4 eggs
- 300g of fresh spinach
- 2 garlic cloves, minced
- Extra virgin olive oil
- Salt and pepper to taste

Preparation:

1. Start by preparing the spinach. Rinse them thoroughly under cold water to remove any soil residues. Drain and set aside.

2. Heat a large pan over medium heat and add a drizzle of olive oil.

3. Add the minced garlic to the pan and sauté for about 1 minute, until it starts to release its aroma.

4. Add the spinach to the pan and mix well to coat with the oil and garlic. Continue to cook until the spinach wilts and reduces in volume. This will take about 3-4 minutes. Season with salt and pepper to taste.

5. Meanwhile, bring a pot of water to a boil and add a pinch of salt.

6. Gently break an egg into a separate cup. Then, create a whirlpool in the boiling water with a spoon and gently pour the egg into the whirlpool. This will help to keep the egg together during cooking. Repeat the process with the other three eggs.

7. Cook the poached eggs for about 3-4 minutes, until the yolks are still soft but the whites are set. You can cook them longer if you prefer firmer yolks.

8. Once cooked, use a slotted spoon to gently remove the eggs from the pot and drain them on a paper towel to dry slightly.

9. Arrange the sautéed spinach on a serving plate and place the poached eggs on top.

10. Add a sprinkle of fresh salt and pepper on the eggs and, if desired, you can finish the dish with a drizzle of extra virgin olive oil.

11. The Poached Eggs on Sautéed Spinach are ready to be enjoyed! Serve warm and savor the delightful combination of flavors and textures.

Poached Eggs on Sautéed Spinach is a dish that combines simplicity with taste. The poached eggs, with their soft and runny yolk, pair perfectly with the sautéed spinach, adding a touch of freshness and nutrients. This dish is ideal for a healthy breakfast, a light lunch, or even a quick dinner. Prepare them to follow our recipe and delight your palate with this delicious flavor combination.

8.Keto Smoothie Bowl with Nuts and Seeds

The Keto Smoothie Bowl with Nuts and Seeds is a refreshing and nourishing breakfast or snack, perfect for those on a ketogenic diet. This delightful bowl is rich in healthy fats, fibers, and proteins, thanks to the nuts and seeds used in its preparation. With its creamy consistency and a mix of flavors and textures, this smoothie bowl will satisfy with every spoonful. Follow our recipe to prepare this keto smoothie bowl and kick-start your day with delicious flavor and optimal nutrition.

Ingredients:

- 1 ripe avocado
- 1/2 cup unsweetened coconut milk
- 1/4 cup mixed nuts (walnuts, almonds, pecans, etc.)
- 1 tablespoon chia seeds
- 1 tablespoon flax seeds
- 1 tablespoon almond or peanut butter
- 1 teaspoon sweetener of choice (stevia, erythritol, xylitol)
- Fresh fruit or seeds for garnishing (optional)

Instructions:

1. Cut the avocado in half, remove the pit, and scoop out the flesh. Place it in a high-powered blender or mixer.

2. Add coconut milk, mixed nuts, chia seeds, flax seeds, almond or peanut butter, and your choice of sweetener to the blender.

3. Blend all ingredients until you achieve a smooth and creamy consistency. If needed, add a bit more coconut milk or water to reach the desired consistency.

4. Pour your keto smoothie bowl into a serving bowl.

5. Garnish with fresh fruit or seeds as desired, such as raspberries, blueberries, pumpkin seeds, or sunflower seeds.

6. Now, you can enjoy your Keto Smoothie Bowl with Nuts and Seeds! Grab a spoon and enjoy this delicious and healthy breakfast that will give you the energy you need for the day.

The Keto Smoothie Bowl with Nuts and Seeds is a delicious and healthy option for breakfast or a snack. Rich in healthy fats, fiber, and protein, thanks to the avocado, nuts, and seeds used, this bowl will provide you with optimal nutritional intake. The creamy texture and the mix of flavors and textures make this smoothie bowl irresistible. Customize the topping with your favorite fresh fruit or seeds and enjoy every spoonful of this ketogenic delicacy. Prepare it following our recipe and start the day with a delicious taste and a burst of energy!

9.Chia and Coconut Keto Pudding

The Chia and Coconut Keto Pudding is a delicious and healthy treat perfectly suited for a ketogenic diet. Made with chia seeds and coconut milk, this pudding is rich in fiber, healthy fats, and antioxidants. With a creamy texture and a slightly sweet taste, this keto pudding is perfect as a dessert or as a nutritionally dense snack. Follow our recipe to prepare this simple and satisfying keto pudding.

Ingredients:

- 1/4 cup chia seeds
- 1 cup unsweetened coconut milk
- 1 teaspoon sweetener of choice (stevia, erythritol, xylitol)
- 1 teaspoon vanilla extract (optional)
- Fresh fruit or grated coconut for garnish (optional)

Instructions:

1. In a bowl, combine chia seeds, coconut milk, sweetener, and vanilla extract (if desired). Mix well to combine the ingredients.
2. Let the mixture sit for 5 minutes, then stir again to ensure even distribution of chia seeds.
3. Cover the bowl with plastic wrap and refrigerate. Allow the pudding to set in the refrigerator for at least 2 hours, or preferably overnight.
4. After resting, remove the keto pudding from the fridge and stir well to break any lumps and achieve a smooth, creamy consistency.
5. Transfer the pudding into serving bowls or jars and garnish with fresh fruit or grated coconut, if desired.
6. Your Chia and Coconut Keto Pudding is ready to be enjoyed! Serve it cold and savor this nutritionally dense treat that won't compromise your ketogenic diet.

The Keto Chia Seed and Coconut Pudding is ready to be enjoyed! Serve it cold and delight in this nutrient-dense sweetness that will please you without compromising your ketogenic diet.

The Keto Chia Seed and Coconut Pudding is a nutritious and delicious dessert that fits perfectly into a ketogenic diet. Made with chia seeds and coconut milk, this pudding offers a combination of fiber, healthy fats, and antioxidants. With a creamy texture and a mildly sweet flavor, it's a perfect choice for a dessert or a nutrient-dense snack. Personalize the pudding with your favorite fresh fruit or shredded coconut for an even more appealing presentation. Prepare it following our recipe and enjoy this healthy treat that will satisfy you without impacting your ketogenic diet.

10. Keto Ricotta Pancakes

Keto Ricotta Pancakes are a light and fluffy option for a delightful snack or breakfast. Made with ricotta and almond flour, these pancakes are rich in flavor and low in carbs. To add a touch of sweetness, they're served with a berry syrup. Follow our step-by-step recipe to savor this ketogenic delicacy!

Ingredients:

- 250g ricotta
- 4 eggs
- 100g almond flour
- 1 teaspoon baking powder
- 1 teaspoon vanilla extract
- Berry syrup for garnishing

Instructions:

1. In a large bowl, mix the ricotta with the eggs until smooth.
2. Add the almond flour, baking powder, and vanilla extract to the ricotta and egg mixture. Mix well to combine all ingredients.
3. Heat a non-stick skillet over medium-low heat and lightly grease it with oil or butter.
4. Pour a ladle of batter into the skillet to form a round pancake. Cook multiple pancakes at once, ensuring there's enough space between them.
5. Cook the pancakes for about 2-3 minutes on each side or until they're golden and puffy.
6. Repeat the process until all the batter is used, adding oil or butter to the skillet when needed.
7. Transfer the pancakes to a serving plate and let them cool slightly.
8. Before serving, drizzle the pancakes with berry syrup for an added touch of sweetness.
9. Your Keto Ricotta Pancakes are ready to be savored! Serve them as a healthy snack or a delicious low-carb breakfast.

The Keto Ricotta Pancakes are incredibly light and fluffy due to the use of ricotta and almond flour. The soft texture and delicate flavor make them a perfect choice for a ketogenic breakfast or snack. The touch of berry syrup adds a note of sweetness that pairs perfectly with the pancakes. Try them and enjoy a guilt-free moment of pleasure!

CHAPTER 6 Lunch Recipes

1.Zucchini Pappardelle with Sundried Tomato and Almond Pesto

Zucchini Pappardelle with Sundried Tomato and Almond Pesto is a creative alternative to classic pappardelle, using thin zucchini strips and a flavorful pesto made with sundried tomatoes and almonds. This delight is fresh, light, and full of Mediterranean flavors.

Ingredients:

- 2 large zucchinis
- 50g sundried tomatoes (soaked in hot water)
- 30g almonds
- 1 garlic clove
- 50ml olive oil
- Salt and pepper, to taste

Instructions:

1. Prepare zucchini pappardelle: Use a spiralizer or vegetable peeler to slice zucchinis into thin strips resembling pappardelle. Set aside.

2. Prepare the sundried tomato and almond pesto: In a blender or food processor, combine drained soaked sundried tomatoes, almonds, garlic clove, and olive oil. Blend until a thick sauce forms. Season with salt and pepper as needed.

3. Toss zucchini pappardelle with pesto: Coat zucchini strips well with the sundried tomato and almond pesto.

4. Serve: Transfer to a serving dish and garnish with some chopped almonds and fresh basil leaves, if desired.

The Zucchini Pappardelle with Sun-dried Tomato and Almond Pesto are ready to be enjoyed! This light alternative to traditional pasta offers a delicious combination of Mediterranean flavors. Perfect to serve as a main dish or as a tasty side.

2. Konjac Spaghetti with Shrimp, Cherry Tomatoes, and Garlic

This konjac spaghetti dish is a great low-carb option. Paired with juicy shrimp, cherry tomatoes, and garlic, it creates a flavorful and healthy meal.

Ingredients:

- 200g konjac spaghetti
- 200g peeled and deveined shrimp
- 150g cherry tomatoes, halved
- 2 garlic cloves, finely minced
- 2 tbsp olive oil
- Dried red chili flakes (optional)
- Fresh parsley, chopped
- Salt and pepper, to taste

Instructions:

1. Drain and rinse konjac spaghetti under cold water, following package instructions.
2. In a large skillet, heat olive oil and sauté minced garlic and red chili flakes (if you want some heat).
3. Add shrimp to the skillet and cook until they turn pink and are fully cooked.
4. Add halved cherry tomatoes and cook for a few minutes until they soften.
5. Mix in konjac spaghetti, ensuring they absorb the flavors well. Season with salt and pepper.
6. Sprinkle chopped parsley over the spaghetti before serving.

The konjac spaghetti with shrimp, cherry tomatoes, and garlic is a delicious option for a light and healthy lunch. Enjoy this combination of Mediterranean flavors!

3.Chickpea Pasta with Eggplant Parmigiana

This dish offers a delicious twist on the classic eggplant parmigiana, combining it with chickpea pasta to create a nutritious and appetizing meal. The soft slices of eggplant, al dente chickpea pasta, and melted cheese layer to form a symphony of Mediterranean flavors. Tomato sauce with garlic adds a flavorful touch that harmonizes all ingredients. This recipe is perfect for those wanting to explore new tastes while retaining a foundation of traditional flavors. Enjoy this Chickpea Pasta with Eggplant Parmigiana and be swept away by the scents and flavors of Mediterranean cuisine.

Ingredients:

- 200 g of chickpea pasta
- 2 medium eggplants, thinly sliced
- 500 ml of tomato sauce
- 2 garlic cloves, finely minced
- 200 g mozzarella, diced
- 50 g grated Parmigiano cheese
- Extra virgin olive oil
- Fresh basil, chopped
- Salt and pepper to taste

Preparation:

1. Preheat the oven to 200°C (390°F).

2. Cook the chickpea pasta in salted boiling water, following package instructions. Drain it al dente and set aside.

3. In a skillet, heat some olive oil and add the eggplant slices. Cook until they become soft and slightly golden on both sides. Set aside.

4. In the same skillet, add some olive oil and the minced garlic. Sauté the garlic for a few minutes until it becomes slightly golden.

5. Add the tomato sauce to the skillet with the garlic, season with salt and pepper to taste, and let it simmer on medium-low heat for about 10-15 minutes until the sauce thickens.

6. In a baking dish, layer some cooked chickpea pasta. Cover with some eggplant slices and diced mozzarella. Sprinkle some grated Parmigiano cheese.

7. Repeat the layering process with pasta, eggplant, mozzarella, and Parmigiano until all ingredients are used.

8. Pour the tomato sauce over the pasta and eggplant layers in the baking dish.

9. Bake the Chickpea Pasta and Eggplant Parmigiana for about 20-25 minutes, or until the cheese turns golden and melted.

10. Once out of the oven, sprinkle the surface with chopped fresh basil before serving.

Chickpea Pasta with Eggplant Parmigiana is a hearty and delicious dish, merging the goodness of chickpea pasta with classic eggplant parmigiana flavors. Bon appétit!

4.Cabbage Lasagna with Meat Ragù and Ricotta

Cabbage Lasagna with Meat Ragù and Ricotta is an innovative and flavorful way to enjoy a classic Italian dish in a keto-Mediterranean version. Instead of pasta, we'll use tender cabbage leaves to create the lasagna layers. The rich and flavorful meat sauce combines with creamy ricotta, offering an irresistible blend of taste and texture. This recipe is perfect for family dinners or to surprise your guests with a gluten-free and flavor-packed dish.

Ingredients:

- 1 large green cabbage, leaves detached and blanched
- 500 g ground meat (beef or pork)
- 1 onion, minced
- 2 garlic cloves, finely minced
- 500 ml of tomato sauce
- 250 g ricotta cheese
- 100 g grated Parmigiano cheese
- Extra virgin olive oil
- Fresh parsley, chopped
- Salt and pepper to taste

Preparation:

1. In a large pot, bring salted water to a boil. Blanch the cabbage leaves for a few minutes until they become soft. Drain and set aside.

2. In a sizable skillet, heat some olive oil and sauté the minced onion and garlic until golden.

3. Add the ground meat to the skillet and cook until it is well browned. Season with salt and pepper.

4. Add the tomato sauce and let it simmer on medium-low heat for about 20-25 minutes until the meat sauce becomes thick and flavorful.

5. In the meantime, preheat the oven to 180°C (350°F).

6. Assembly: In a slightly greased baking dish, place a layer of blanched cabbage leaves. Cover with a layer of meat ragù and spoonfuls of ricotta. Sprinkle with grated Parmigiano cheese. Continue layering until all ingredients are used, ensuring you end with some grated cheese on top.

7. Bake the Cabbage Lasagna for about 30-35 minutes or until the surface becomes golden and crispy.

8. Once out of the oven, sprinkle with chopped fresh parsley before serving.

Cabbage Lasagna with Meat Ragù and Ricotta is a tasty gluten-free option to relish a classic Italian recipe while following the keto-Mediterranean diet. Bon appétit!

5. Cucumber Pappardelle with Avocado Sauce and Smoked Salmon

Cucumber Pappardelle with Avocado Sauce and Smoked Salmon is a refreshing and tasty option for those on a keto-Mediterranean diet. The cucumber is thinly sliced to create "pappardelle" that are fresh and light. The creamy avocado sauce and smoked salmon provide a delicate and nutritious touch of flavor. This dish is ideal for warm days and as a carb-free option for those looking to stay in shape without compromising taste.

Ingredients:

- 2 long cucumbers
- 1 ripe avocado
- Juice of 1 lemon
- 100 g thinly sliced smoked salmon
- Fresh parsley, chopped
- Salt and pepper to taste

Preparation:

1. Slice the cucumbers lengthwise using a vegetable peeler or mandolin to create thin pappardelle-like strips. Set aside.

2. In a bowl, mash the ripe avocado with a fork and add the lemon juice. Mix until you achieve a creamy sauce. Season with salt and pepper to taste.

3. Avocado Sauce: Add the cucumber pappardelle to the bowl with the avocado sauce and gently toss until the cucumber strips are well coated.

4. To serve, garnish the Cucumber Pappardelle with slices of smoked salmon and a sprinkle of fresh parsley.

Cucumber Pappardelle with Avocado Sauce and Smoked Salmon is a refreshing and healthy dish, perfect for warm days or as a light alternative to traditional pasta.

6.Pasta Frittata with Zucchini and Goat Cheese

The "Pasta Frittata with Zucchini and Goat Cheese" is a delicacy from the keto-Mediterranean cuisine that combines the convenience of leftover pasta with the freshness of zucchini and the creaminess of goat cheese. This thick and fluffy frittata is a complete and tasty meal, perfect for breakfast, lunch, or a light dinner.

Ingredients:

- 200 g of leftover pasta (any type of pasta of your choice)
- 2 medium zucchinis, thinly sliced
- 100 g of soft goat cheese, crumbled
- 6 large eggs
- 50 ml of milk (or almond milk for a lactose-free version)
- 1 medium onion, finely chopped
- 2 tablespoons of olive oil
- Salt and pepper to taste
- Fresh parsley, chopped (optional, for garnish)

Preparation:

1. In a large bowl, beat the eggs with the milk and a pinch of salt and pepper. Add the leftover pasta and mix well to ensure it's completely coated with the egg mixture.

2. In a non-stick pan about 25 cm in diameter, heat the olive oil over medium heat. Add the finely chopped onion and zucchini slices and cook until they become soft and slightly golden. Set them aside.

3. In the same pan, add some more olive oil if needed, and pour in the egg and pasta mixture. Level the surface with a spoon to evenly distribute the ingredients.

4. Scatter the crumbled goat cheese on top and cover the pan with a lid.

5. Cook the frittata over medium-low heat for about 8-10 minutes or until the bottom becomes golden and the top appears partially dry.

6. At this point, flip the frittata onto a flat plate or use a lid to help slide the frittata out of the pan. Then, gently slide the frittata back into the pan to cook the other side.

7. Continue cooking for another 6-8 minutes or until both sides are golden and the frittata is firm and fully cooked.

8. Sprinkle the frittata with chopped fresh parsley, if desired, before serving.

The "Pasta Frittata with Zucchini and Goat Cheese" is ready to enjoy! Slice it into wedges and serve warm, perhaps accompanied by a fresh green salad for a complete and delightful meal.

7. Legume Penne with Eggplant Sauce and Salted Ricotta

The "Legume Penne with Eggplant Sauce and Salted Ricotta" is a nutritious and tasty option for those following the keto-Mediterranean diet. This legume-based pasta, rich in protein and low in carbs, is paired with a delicious eggplant and tomato sauce, giving the dish a rich and savory flavor. The salted ricotta, with its salty and creamy taste, adds an irresistible final touch.

Ingredients:

- 250 g of legume penne (e.g., chickpea or lentil penne)
- 2 medium eggplants, cubed
- 400 g of diced tomatoes (preferably peeled)
- 2 cloves of garlic, finely chopped
- 1 medium onion, finely chopped
- 50 g of salted ricotta, grated
- Fresh basil, chopped
- Extra virgin olive oil
- Salt and pepper to taste

Preparation:

1. In a large pot, bring a generous amount of salted water to a boil and cook the legume penne according to the package instructions. Drain them al dente and set aside.

2. In a large pan, heat a drizzle of olive oil and add the finely chopped garlic and onion. Sauté over medium-high heat until golden.

3. Add the eggplant cubes to the pan and cook until they become soft and slightly golden.

4. Add the diced tomatoes to the pan with the eggplants and season with salt and pepper to taste. Let it simmer over medium-low heat for about 15-20 minutes until the tomato sauce becomes thick and flavorful.

5. Add the legume penne to the eggplant sauce and gently mix to combine the ingredients.

6. Serve the penne with the eggplant sauce and sprinkle the grated salted ricotta on top.

7. Garnish with chopped fresh basil leaves before serving.

This recipe offers a combination of Mediterranean flavors, with the richness of eggplants and tomatoes, and the added protein from the legume penne.

8.Cauliflower Risotto with Shrimp and Saffron

This recipe is a delicacy inspired by Mediterranean cuisine, combining the creaminess of risotto with the delicate taste of cauliflower and shrimp. The distinctive touch of saffron adds a refined flavor note and a golden color to the dish. This recipe is perfect for those who wish to enjoy a risotto without rice, while still retaining the aroma and consistency of a classic risotto.

Ingredients:

- 1 medium cauliflower, cut into small florets
- 300g of fresh shrimp, peeled and deveined
- 1 medium onion, finely chopped
- 2 cloves of garlic, finely chopped
- 300g of risotto rice (or cauliflower rice for a completely carb-free version)
- 500ml of hot vegetable broth
- 1 sachet of saffron (about 0.1g) or some saffron threads
- 50ml of dry white wine
- 50g of butter or extra virgin olive oil
- Grated Parmesan cheese (optional)
- Salt and pepper to taste
- Fresh parsley, chopped (for garnish)

Preparation:

1. In a large pot, bring plenty of salted water to a boil. Add the cauliflower florets and blanch for a few minutes until they are tender yet still crisp. Drain the cauliflower and set aside.

2. In a large pan, heat the butter or olive oil over medium heat. Add the chopped onion and garlic and sauté until golden.

3. Add the shrimp to the pan and cook until they turn pink and are well-cooked. Set aside.

4. In the same pan, add the risotto rice and lightly toast it until it becomes translucent.

5. Pour the white wine into the pan and let it evaporate, continuously stirring the rice.

6. Add a ladle of hot vegetable broth to the rice and stir until the liquid is absorbed. Continue adding the broth, one ladle at a time, while stirring, until the rice is creamy and al dente (about 15-18 minutes).

7. Stir in the saffron threads until the rice acquires the saffron's golden color.

8. Add the blanched cauliflower and the cooked shrimp to the pan with the rice and gently mix to combine all the ingredients.

9. Taste the risotto and season with salt and pepper as desired.

10. If desired, sprinkle the risotto with grated Parmesan cheese and garnish with chopped fresh parsley before serving.

This Mediterranean delight offers a combination of delicate and refined flavors, with the earthiness of cauliflower, the delicacy of sea shrimp, and the luxurious touch of saffron.

9.Tomato and Basil Soup with Buffalo Mozzarella

Ingredients:

- 800g of ripe tomatoes, peeled and diced
- 1 medium onion, finely chopped
- 2 cloves of garlic, chopped
- 4 tablespoons of extra virgin olive oil
- 1 teaspoon of tomato paste
- 500ml of vegetable broth
- 1 bunch of fresh basil
- 200g of buffalo mozzarella, diced
- Freshly ground black pepper and salt to taste

Preparation:

1. In a large pot, heat two tablespoons of extra virgin olive oil over medium heat. Add the chopped onion and let it wilt for a few minutes until translucent.

2. Add the chopped garlic cloves to the onion and cook for another minute until they release their fragrant aroma.

3. Add the diced tomatoes and tomato paste to the pot. Mix well and cook for 5-7 minutes until the tomatoes soften.

4. Pour the vegetable broth into the pot, bring to a boil, and then reduce the heat to low-medium. Add half of the fresh basil leaves and let the soup simmer for about 15-20 minutes, allowing the flavors to blend.

5. In the meantime, season the buffalo mozzarella cubes with a pinch of salt and pepper.

6. When the soup is ready, blend it with an immersion blender until smooth and velvety.

7. Pour the tomato and basil soup into individual bowls. Top with the buffalo mozzarella cubes and remaining basil leaves for garnish.

The Tomato and Basil Soup with Buffalo Mozzarella is a true explosion of Mediterranean flavors. The freshness of the tomatoes and basil combined with the creaminess of the buffalo mozzarella creates a symphony of taste with every spoonful. The aroma of the extra virgin olive oil emphasizes the authenticity of this keto-Mediterranean soup, perfect for satisfying anyone's palate, even on a low-carb diet. Serve it hot, perhaps accompanied by keto bread croutons, and you'll win everyone over with this delicious and healthy dish.

10. Herb Chicken with Olives and Sun-Dried Tomatoes

Herb Chicken with Olives and Sun-Dried Tomatoes is a dish from the Mediterranean cuisine that enchants with its combination of intense and aromatic flavors. The scent of fresh herbs, such as rosemary, sage, and thyme, marries the sweetness of sun-dried tomatoes and the savoriness of black olives, creating a symphony of flavors in every bite. The tender chicken breast meat becomes succulent when cooked in extra virgin olive oil, making this dish a true delight for the palate. Easy to prepare, Herb Chicken with Olives and Sun-Dried Tomatoes is perfect for a special lunch or dinner, or simply to indulge in a flavorful and nutritious Mediterranean dish.

Ingredients:

- 4 boneless, skinless chicken breasts
- 2 tablespoons extra virgin olive oil
- 2 garlic cloves, finely chopped
- 1 teaspoon fresh rosemary, chopped
- 1 teaspoon fresh sage, chopped
- 1 teaspoon fresh thyme, chopped
- 1/2 teaspoon dried red chili pepper (optional)
- 1/2 cup pitted black olives
- 1/4 cup sun-dried tomatoes in oil, chopped.
- 1/2 cup chicken broth
- Salt and freshly ground black pepper, to taste.

Preparation:

1. Preheat the oven to 200°C (390°F).

2. In a large skillet, heat the extra virgin olive oil over medium-high heat. Add the finely chopped garlic cloves and sauté them until they release their fragrant aroma.

3. Add the chicken breasts to the skillet and cook them for 4-5 minutes on each side, until they turn golden.

4. Add the chopped aromatic herbs (rosemary, sage, and thyme) to the chicken. If you wish to add a touch of spiciness, you can also include the dried red chili pepper.

5. Reduce the heat to medium-low and add the pitted black olives and chopped sun-dried tomatoes to the skillet.

6. Pour the chicken broth into the skillet, cover it with a lid, and cook for another 10-12 minutes, or until the chicken is fully cooked and the broth has slightly reduced.

7. Taste and adjust with salt and pepper according to your preferences.

8. Transfer the herb chicken with olives and sun-dried tomatoes to a serving dish. You can garnish with a few sprigs of fresh herbs for a final touch.

This dish is rich in Mediterranean flavors that will delight your senses. The aromatic herbs, olives, and sun-dried tomatoes harmoniously blend to create a tasty and satisfying taste. Serve the chicken with a side of grilled vegetables or a fresh salad for a complete and healthy meal. Enjoy your meal!

CHAPTER 7 Dinner Recipes

1.Grilled Beef Steak with Arugula and Parmesan

The Grilled Beef Steak with Arugula and Parmesan is an irresistible dish that combines intense and genuine flavors. The beef, cooked to perfection, is complemented by the freshness of arugula and the aromaticity of parmesan, creating a unique taste combination. The meat, sliced thinly and cooked just right, blends with the bold taste of arugula and the elegance of parmesan, offering an unforgettable culinary experience. The simplicity of this dish makes it ideal for a special lunch or dinner, where you can delight your guests with a heartwarming Italian dish.

Ingredients:

- 500 g of beef steak
- 100 g of fresh arugula
- 50 g of Parmigiano Reggiano, grated or thinly sliced
- 2 tablespoons of extra virgin olive oil
- Juice of 1 lemon
- Salt and freshly ground black pepper, to taste

Preparation:

1. First, bring the beef steak to room temperature by letting it rest outside the fridge for at least 30 minutes.

2. Heat the grill or set it to high heat, making sure it's very hot.

3. Season the beef steak with salt and freshly ground black pepper on both sides. You can also brush it lightly with olive oil to prevent sticking to the grill.

4. Grill the meat for 3-5 minutes on each side, depending on your preferred level of doneness (rare, medium, or well-done).

5. Once cooked, remove the beef steak from the grill and let it rest for a few minutes on a cutting board.

6. Meanwhile, in a bowl, prepare the vinaigrette by mixing the extra virgin olive oil and lemon juice. Adjust salt and pepper if needed.

7. Slice the beef steak thinly, arrange it on a serving dish, and drizzle with the prepared vinaigrette.

8. Add fresh arugula over the meat and finish the dish with grated or sliced Parmigiano Reggiano.

The Grilled Beef Steak with Arugula and Parmesan is a triumph of Italian flavors that will captivate your senses. The tender and succulent beef perfectly complements the vibrant arugula and the intense flavor of Parmigiano Reggiano, creating a perfect balance between sweetness, freshness, and robustness. This dish, highlighted by the simplicity of the olive oil and lemon vinaigrette, is a tribute to Mediterranean cuisine and a true delight for anyone tasting it. Serve the Grilled Beef Steak with Arugula and Parmesan alongside grilled vegetables or roasted potatoes for a complete and irresistible meal.

2. Baked Salmon with Olive and Caper Sauce

The Baked Salmon with Olive and Caper Sauce is a sophisticated and tasty dish that can be prepared in no time. The combination of salmon, olives, and capers gives this recipe a unique Mediterranean flavor, full of aromatic and savory notes. The salmon fillets, baked with a touch of lemon and garlic, become tender and juicy, while the sauce of black olives and capers enhances the fish's taste with its bold character. The fresh parsley adds a touch of freshness to the sauce, completing this dish with a hint of color and fragrance. The Baked Salmon with Olive and Caper Sauce is perfect for an elegant dinner or a special meal with friends and family. Try it and be captivated by the goodness of Mediterranean flavors.

Ingredients:

- 4 salmon fillets, skinless
- 2 tablespoons of extra virgin olive oil
- Juice of 1 lemon
- 2 garlic cloves, finely minced
- 1/4 cup of pitted black olives, chopped
- 2 tablespoons of capers, rinsed and drained
- 1 tablespoon of fresh parsley, chopped
- Salt and freshly ground black pepper, to taste

Preparation:

1. Preheat the oven to 200°C (390°F).

2. In a small bowl, mix the extra virgin olive oil with the lemon juice, minced garlic, and a pinch of salt and pepper.

3. Place the salmon fillets in a baking dish and brush them with the flavored olive oil mixture.

4. Bake the salmon in the preheated oven for about 12-15 minutes, or until the flesh easily flakes with a fork.

5. In the meantime, prepare the olive and caper sauce. In a skillet, heat a tablespoon of extra virgin olive oil over medium heat. Add the chopped black olives and capers and cook for 2-3 minutes.

6. Remove the skillet from the heat and mix in the chopped parsley.

7. Once the salmon is cooked, remove it from the oven and transfer it to a serving dish.

8. Pour the olive and caper sauce over the salmon, distributing it evenly.

The Baked Salmon with Olive and Caper Sauce is a recipe that wonderfully enhances the flavor of the salmon. The oven baking keeps the fish's flesh soft and juicy, while the olive and caper sauce adds an irresistible Mediterranean touch. The delicate taste of the salmon perfectly pairs with the bold flavor of the olives and the briny note of the capers, creating a harmonious and satisfying dish. Serve this delicacy with a side of fresh vegetables or a bed of mashed potatoes for a complete and healthy meal.

3. Almond Chicken with Crunchy Vegetables

The Almond Chicken with Crunchy Vegetables is a delicious dish that combines the delicate taste of chicken with the crispiness of almonds and the freshness of vegetables. Chicken breasts, carefully breaded with almond flour and breadcrumbs, are cooked to perfection, resulting in juicy and flavorful meat. The crispy vegetables, cut into sticks and strips, add a colorful and healthy touch to the dish. Everything is enriched with a delightful Greek yogurt and lemon sauce, adding a fresh and tangy note to the Almond Chicken with Crunchy Vegetables. This delicacy is ideal for a special dinner or to surprise guests with a tasty and original Mediterranean dish. Prepare it for an unforgettable evening with your loved ones, and let yourself be won over by this unique combination of flavors and textures.

Ingredients:

- 4 chicken breasts, skinless and boneless
- 1/2 cup almond flour
- 2 eggs
- 1/2 cup breadcrumbs
- 1 teaspoon paprika
- Salt and freshly ground black pepper, to taste
- 2 tablespoons extra virgin olive oil

For the crunchy vegetables:

- 2 carrots, cut into thin sticks
- 1 zucchini, sliced
- 1 red bell pepper, cut into strips
- 1 yellow bell pepper, cut into strips
- 1 tablespoon extra virgin olive oil
- Salt and freshly ground black pepper

To taste Sauce:

- 1/4 cup Greek yogurt
- Juice of 1 lemon
- 1 garlic clove, finely chopped
- Fresh parsley, chopped, to taste

Preparation:

1. Set up a breading station for the chicken by filling three separate dishes: one with the almond flour, one with the beaten eggs, and one with the breadcrumbs mixed with paprika, salt, and pepper.

2. Coat each chicken breast first in the almond flour, then the beaten eggs, and finally in the breadcrumbs, making sure to cover each side well. Set the breaded chicken aside.

3. Prepare the crunchy vegetables: in a large skillet, heat a tablespoon of olive oil over medium-high heat. Add the carrots, zucchini, and bell peppers, cooking until they're slightly tender yet still crisp. Season with salt and pepper to taste. Remove the vegetables from the pan and set them aside.

4. In the same skillet, add another tablespoon of olive oil and cook the breaded chicken breasts over medium-high heat for about 4-5 minutes on each side, or until they are golden brown and cooked through.

5. While the chicken cooks, prepare the sauce by mixing the Greek yogurt, lemon juice, chopped garlic, and fresh parsley. Stir until you have a creamy and smooth sauce.

6. Once cooked, remove the chicken breasts from the skillet and place them on a serving dish.

7. Arrange the crunchy vegetables around the chicken and garnish with chopped fresh parsley.

8. Serve the Almond Chicken with Crunchy Vegetables with a generous dollop of the yogurt and lemon sauce on the side.

This Almond Chicken with Crispy Vegetables dish is an explosion of flavors and textures. The crunchiness of the almond-floured breaded chicken combines with the freshness and lightness of the stir-fried vegetables, while the yogurt and lemon sauce add a creamy and tangy note to everything. A tasty and healthy meal that will win over the palate of all diners.

4.Stuffed Peppers with Quinoa and Feta Cheese

The Stuffed Peppers with Quinoa and Feta Cheese, suitable for the keto-Mediterranean diet, are a tasty and healthy option that combines the protein richness of quinoa with the creamy taste of feta cheese. This recipe is ideal for those looking to maintain a low-carb diet without sacrificing a flavorful and nutrient-rich meal. The bell peppers, with their sweet flavor and tender texture, serve as a perfect vessel for the delightful quinoa and feta cheese filling.

Ingredients:

- 4 large bell peppers (red, yellow, or orange)
- 1 cup quinoa, well rinsed
- 2 cups low-sodium vegetable broth
- 1 small onion, finely chopped
- 2 garlic cloves, finely chopped
- 1 small zucchini, diced
- 1 ripe tomato, diced
- 1/2 cup crumbled feta cheese
- 2 tablespoons extra virgin olive oil
- 1 teaspoon dried oregano
- Salt and freshly ground black pepper, to taste
- Fresh parsley, chopped, for garnish

Preparation:

1. Preheat the oven to 200°C (390°F).

2. Cut the top off each bell pepper and remove the seeds and inner membranes. Rinse the peppers under cold water and set them aside.

3. In a pot, bring the low-sodium vegetable broth to a boil. Add the quinoa and a pinch of salt. Reduce the heat to medium-low, cover, and let the quinoa cook for about 15-20 minutes, or until it's slightly tender and all the broth has been absorbed. Drain if necessary.

4. In a large skillet, heat the olive oil over medium heat. Add the finely chopped onion and garlic, sautéing until they become translucent and aromatic.

5. Add the diced zucchini to the skillet and cook for 3-4 minutes until it softens.

6. Stir in the diced tomato and let it cook for another 2-3 minutes.

7. Combine the cooked quinoa with the vegetables in the skillet and mix well. Season with dried oregano, salt, and freshly ground black pepper to taste. Ensure all ingredients are well blended.

8. Fill the bell peppers with the quinoa and vegetable mixture, pressing down slightly to compact it.

9. Place the stuffed peppers in a baking dish lightly greased with olive oil.

10. Bake the stuffed peppers in the preheated oven for about 20-25 minutes, or until the peppers become soft and slightly golden.

11. During the last 5 minutes of baking, sprinkle the crumbled feta cheese over the top of each stuffed pepper, allowing it to melt slightly.

12. Once cooked, remove the stuffed peppers from the oven and garnish with chopped fresh parsley.

The Stuffed Peppers with Quinoa and Feta Cheese, suitable for the keto-mediterranean diet, are a delicious combination of flavors and nutrients. Quinoa provides a source of protein and fiber without increasing the carbs, while the feta cheese, rich in good fats and protein, contributes to making the dish creamy and flavorful. This colorful and appetizing dish is perfect for a balanced and tasty dinner, also ideal for those following a low-carb diet. Serve the stuffed peppers as a main dish with a salad of leafy greens or with a serving of avocado to complete a satisfying keto-mediterranean dinner. Delight your diners with this delicacy suitable for your diet and enjoy a healthy and flavorful dinner.

5. Shrimp and Asparagus Pan-Seared with Garlic Lemon Butter

This keto-Mediterranean delight combines the delicacy of shrimp with the fresh, crisp taste of asparagus. The garlic lemon butter adds richness and flavor, crafting a balanced and tasty dish. This recipe is perfect for an elegant dinner or a quick, healthy meal, satisfying even the most refined palates.

Ingredients:

- 500g fresh shrimp, peeled and cleaned
- 1 bunch of asparagus, tips cut and lower part peeled
- 3 tablespoons unsalted butter
- 2 garlic cloves, finely chopped
- Juice and zest of 1 lemon
- Fresh parsley, chopped
- Salt and freshly ground black pepper, to taste
- Red chili pepper (optional)

Preparation:

1. In a large non-stick skillet, melt butter over medium-low heat.
2. Add the chopped garlic to the skillet and sauté for a few minutes until fragrant.
3. Add asparagus to the skillet and cook for about 5 minutes until they are tender but still crisp. Season with salt and pepper.
4. Add the peeled shrimp to the skillet with the asparagus and cook for 2-3 minutes on each side or until shrimp turn pink and are fully cooked.
5. Squeeze lemon juice over the shrimp and asparagus, and add the lemon zest for a refreshing touch.
6. Stir in the chopped parsley and mix well.
7. If you enjoy some heat, add some chopped red chili pepper.
8. Remove shrimp and asparagus from the skillet and plate.
9. Garnish with some more chopped fresh parsley and additional lemon zest if desired.

Shrimp and Asparagus in Garlic Lemon Butter are an explosion of perfectly balanced flavors and textures. The tenderness of the shrimp pairs perfectly with the crispness of the asparagus, while the garlic lemon butter adds a touch of richness and freshness to the dish. This recipe is a great option for a quick dinner that is sure to impress. The vibrant colors of the asparagus and shrimp will capture the attention of your diners, while the flavor of the garlic lemon butter will leave them satisfied and content. Serve the Shrimp and Asparagus in Garlic Lemon Butter as a main dish with a fresh mixed salad for a complete and tasty keto-mediterranean meal.

6.Grilled Beef Steak with Basil Pesto and Cherry Tomatoes

This succulent dish combines tender beef steak with the freshness of basil pesto and the sweet taste of cherry tomatoes. This keto-Mediterranean recipe is a prime choice for meat lovers and delivers an explosion of Mediterranean flavors.

Ingredients:

- 2 beef steaks (ribeye, sirloin, or your preferred cut)
- Salt and freshly ground black pepper, to taste
- Extra virgin olive oil
- 1 cup fresh basil leaves
- 1/4 cup almonds or pine nuts
- 1/4 cup grated cheese (pecorino or parmesan)
- 2 garlic cloves
- 1/2 cup cherry tomatoes, halved

Preparation:

1. Preheat the grill on medium-high heat.

2. Prepare the basil pesto: In a blender or mixer, combine basil leaves, almonds or pine nuts, grated cheese, and garlic cloves. Blend until smooth. Season with salt and pepper. Add olive oil as needed to achieve desired consistency. Set aside.

3. Season steaks with salt and freshly ground black pepper on both sides.

4. Brush both sides of the steaks with extra virgin olive oil.

5. Place steaks on the hot grill and cook for 3-4 minutes on each side or to your desired doneness. Flip only once for a perfect crust.

6. During the last minute of grilling, place the halved cherry tomatoes on the grill and let them cook briefly until slightly softened.

7. Remove steaks and tomatoes from the grill and place on a serving dish.

8. Drizzle a generous amount of basil pesto over each steak and garnish with grilled cherry tomatoes.

Grilled Beef Steak with Basil Pesto and Cherry Tomatoes is a keto-mediterranean delight that will satisfy the palate of all meat lovers. The beef steak, succulent and flavorful, pairs perfectly with the basil pesto, which adds a touch of freshness and Mediterranean flavor. The grilled cherry tomatoes complete the dish with their sweet and slightly smoky taste. This recipe is perfect for a special dinner or an outdoor barbecue with friends and family. Accompany the steak with a selection of grilled vegetables or a fresh salad for a complete and satisfying keto-mediterranean dinner.

7. Shrimp and Tomato Soup with Fennel and Parsley

The Shrimp and Tomato Soup with Fennel and Parsley is a delicious and flavorful keto-Mediterranean dish, perfect for cool evenings or as comfort food. This soup combines the sweetness of shrimp with the rich and tangy flavor of tomatoes, enriched by the aromatic taste of fennel and parsley. The freshness of parsley gives the soup a touch of color and vitality, making this dish irresistible and nutritious.

Ingredients:

- 500 g of fresh shrimp, peeled and cleaned
- 2 tablespoons of extra virgin olive oil
- 1 medium onion, finely chopped
- 2 garlic cloves, finely chopped
- 2 large fennels, thinly sliced
- 1 can (400 g) of peeled tomatoes, chopped
- 4 cups of fish or low-sodium vegetable broth
- 1/2 cup of dry white wine (optional)
- Salt and freshly ground black pepper, to taste
- Fresh parsley, chopped, for garnish

Preparation:

1. In a large pot, heat the olive oil over medium heat.
2. Add the finely chopped onion and garlic to the pot and sauté until translucent and aromatic.
3. Add the thinly sliced fennel to the pot and cook for 5-6 minutes, until tender.
4. Add the chopped peeled tomatoes to the pot and mix well with the fennel and onions.
5. Pour the fish or vegetable broth into the pot and bring to a boil.
6. Reduce the heat to medium-low and simmer the soup for about 15-20 minutes, allowing the flavors to meld.
7. Add the peeled shrimp to the soup and cook for 3-4 minutes, or until the shrimp turn pink and are fully cooked. If desired, you can add the dry white wine to further enhance the soup's flavors.
8. Taste and adjust the salt and pepper to your liking.
9. Remove the pot from the heat and prepare to serve.

10. Pour the Shrimp and Tomato Soup with Fennel and Parsley into serving bowls and garnish with plenty of chopped fresh parsley.

This Shrimp and Tomato Soup with Fennel and Parsley is a keto-Mediterranean delight that will tantalize your senses with a combination of Mediterranean flavors and aromas. Perfect for a comforting dinner or to share a special meal with friends and family, this soup is a treat for both the palate and the eyes. Serve this Shrimp and Tomato Soup with Fennel and Parsley with a slice of keto-Mediterranean bread or a fresh salad for a complete and satisfying meal.

8.Grilled Tuna with Olive and Caper Sauce

The Grilled Tuna with Olive and Caper Sauce is a keto-Mediterranean dish that captivates with the combination of fresh tuna flavors, the intense taste of olives, and the salty aroma of capers. This recipe offers a unique taste experience, with the grilled tuna perfectly complementing the olive and caper sauce. The grilling of the tuna provides a smoky note, while the sauce creates a perfect harmony of Mediterranean flavors. This dish is a great option for a light yet tasty dinner.

Ingredients:

- 4 slices of fresh tuna fillet
- 2 tablespoons of extra virgin olive oil
- Salt and freshly ground black pepper, to taste
- 1/2 cup of black olives, pitted and sliced
- 2 tablespoons of capers, rinsed and drained
- 2 garlic cloves, finely chopped
- Juice of 1/2 lemon
- Fresh parsley, chopped, for garnish

Preparation:

1. Preheat the grill to medium-high heat.
2. Season the tuna slices with salt and freshly ground black pepper on both sides.
3. Brush both sides of the tuna slices with a bit of extra virgin olive oil.
4. Place the tuna on the hot grill and cook for 2-3 minutes on each side, or until the tuna is cooked but still pink inside. Do not overcook to avoid making it too dry.
5. While the tuna is grilling, prepare the olive and caper sauce. In a small pan, heat a bit of olive oil over medium heat.
6. Add the finely chopped garlic cloves to the pan and sauté until fragrant.
7. Add the sliced olives and capers to the pan with the garlic and cook for 1-2 minutes.
8. Squeeze the lemon juice over the olive and caper sauce and mix well.
9. Remove the olive and caper sauce from the pan and set aside.

10. Remove the grilled tuna from the grill and place it on a serving plate.

11. Pour the olive and caper sauce over the grilled tuna slices.

12. Garnish the dish with chopped fresh parsley.

The Grilled Tuna with Olive and Caper Sauce is a delightful culinary experience that blends the flavors of the sea and the land. The grilled tuna, tender and succulent, pairs perfectly with the olive and caper sauce, adding an intense and aromatic flavor to the dish. The freshness of the parsley adds a touch of color and vitality to the presentation. This dish is ideal for a light yet satisfying dinner, perfect for those looking for a keto-Mediterranean dish that showcases genuine tastes. Serve the Grilled Tuna with Olive and Caper Sauce with a fresh seasonal salad or grilled vegetables for a complete and balanced dinner. Enjoy every bite of this Mediterranean delicacy and let its harmony of flavors win you over.

9. Baked Salmon with Almond and Herb Crust

Baked Salmon with Almond and Herb Crust is a refined and tasty dish that combines the delicacy of salmon with the crunchiness of almonds and the fragrant aroma of herbs. This keto-Mediterranean recipe offers a combination of Mediterranean flavors, with oven-baked salmon perfectly paired with an almond crust and aromatic herbs. The crust gives the salmon a note of flavor and texture, making this dish a perfect choice for an elegant dinner or for sharing a special meal with friends.

Ingredients:

- 4 fresh salmon fillets
- 1 cup chopped almonds
- 2 tablespoons fresh parsley, chopped
- 1 tablespoon fresh thyme, chopped
- 1 tablespoon fresh rosemary, chopped
- 2 tablespoons Dijon mustard
- 2 tablespoons extra virgin olive oil
- Freshly ground salt and black pepper, to taste
- Lemon slices for garnish

Preparation:

1. Preheat the oven to 200°C (390°F) and line a baking tray with parchment paper.

2. In a bowl, mix the chopped almonds with parsley, thyme, and rosemary. Add a pinch of salt and freshly ground black pepper and mix well to evenly distribute the herbs.

3. Brush each salmon fillet with a thin strip of Dijon mustard on both sides.

4. Place the salmon fillets on the prepared baking tray.

5. Press the almond and herb crust onto the salmon fillets, pressing gently to make it adhere.

6. Drizzle a stream of extra virgin olive oil over each salmon fillet.

7. Bake the salmon in the preheated oven for about 12-15 minutes, or until the salmon is cooked and the almond crust is golden and crispy.

8. Remove the salmon from the oven and let it rest for a few minutes before serving.

9. Garnish each salmon fillet with a lemon slice before bringing to the table.

The Baked Salmon with Almond and Herb Crust stands out for the elegance and refinement of its flavors. The salmon, tender and flavorful, pairs perfectly with the almond crust and aromatic herbs, giving the dish a note of crunchiness and fragrance. The Dijon mustard gives the salmon a slight spiciness that harmoniously blends with the almonds. This dish is ideal for a special dinner or to surprise guests with a Mediterranean delight. Serve the Baked Salmon with Almond and Herb Crust with a fresh seasonal salad or a selection of grilled vegetables for a complete and satisfying meal. Enjoy every bite of this delicacy and be transported by the Mediterranean flavors that will delight your senses.

10. Beef Tagliata with Arugula, Cherry Tomatoes, and Parmesan Shavings

Beef Tagliata with Arugula, Cherry Tomatoes, and Parmesan Shavings is an irresistible keto-Mediterranean dish that combines the succulence of beef with the freshness of arugula and the sweetness of cherry tomatoes. Parmesan shavings complete this tasty combination of flavors, creating a dish full of contrasts and harmony.

Ingredients:

- 500g beef tagliata
- Freshly ground salt and black pepper, to taste
- 2 tablespoons extra virgin olive oil
- 4 cups fresh arugula
- 1 cup cherry tomatoes, halved
- Parmesan reggiano shavings, for garnish

Preparation:

1. Preheat the grill or pan over high heat.

2. Season the beef tagliata with freshly ground salt and black pepper on both sides.

3. Brush both sides of the beef tagliata with some extra virgin olive oil.

4. Place the beef tagliata on the hot grill or pan and cook for 2-3 minutes on each side, or until the desired level of doneness is reached. Remember to turn the meat only once to get a nice crust on the surface.

5. Remove the beef tagliata from the grill or pan and let it rest for a few minutes before slicing.

6. Slice the beef tagliata thinly and arrange on a serving dish.

7. In a bowl, dress the arugula with a drizzle of extra virgin olive oil and a light spritz of lemon juice. Mix well.

8. Arrange the arugula over the beef tagliata on the serving dish.

9. Garnish with halved cherry tomatoes and Parmesan reggiano shavings.

The Beef Tagliata with Arugula, Cherry Tomatoes, and Parmesan Shavings enhances the goodness of beef with an explosion of fresh and Mediterranean flavors. The succulent and flavorful beef tagliata harmoniously blends with the freshness of arugula and the sweetness of cherry tomatoes. The Parmesan reggiano shavings complete the dish with a touch of salty and creamy flavor. This recipe is perfect for an elegant dinner, or a meal shared with friends and family. Accompany the Beef Tagliata with Arugula, Cherry Tomatoes, and Parmesan Shavings with a selection of grilled vegetables or a fresh mixed salad for a complete and tasty keto-Mediterranean meal. Enjoy every bite of this delicacy and be transported by the Mediterranean flavors that will delight your senses.

CHAPTER 8 Dessert Recipes

1.Sugar-Free Lemon and Almond Cake

The Sugar-Free Lemon and Almond Cake is a delightful keto-Mediterranean dessert that pleases the palate with the fresh taste of lemon and the crunchiness of almonds. This cake is free from refined sugar but full of flavors and nutrients. The natural sweetness of the lemon and a low-carb sweetener make this cake perfect for those following a low-carb and sugar diet. Make it for a snack or as a dessert for a special dinner and let yourself be won over by Mediterranean flavors.

Ingredients:

- 2 cups of almond flour
- 1/2 cup of erythritol (or another low-carb sweetener)
- 1/2 cup of unsalted butter, melted
- 4 large eggs
- Zest of 2 untreated lemons
- Juice of 2 lemons
- 1 teaspoon of baking powder
- A pinch of salt
- Sliced almonds for garnishing (optional)

Preparation:
1. Preheat the oven to 180°C (350°F) and prepare a cake mold, lining it with parchment paper or greasing it with butter and almond flour.
2. In a large bowl, mix the almond flour, erythritol, baking powder, and a pinch of salt.
3. Add the melted butter to the almond flour mixture and mix until you get a homogeneous mixture.
4. Add the eggs one at a time, mixing well after each addition.
5. Add the grated lemon zest and lemon juice to the mixture and mix until you get a smooth and homogeneous dough.
6. Pour the dough into the prepared pan and level the surface.
7. If desired, sprinkle the surface of the cake with sliced almonds for a crunchy decoration.
8. Bake the cake in the preheated oven for about 25-30 minutes, or until the cake is golden and a toothpick inserted into the center comes out clean.
9. Remove the cake from the oven and let it cool completely before removing it from the mold. The

Sugar-Free Lemon and Almond Cake is an explosion of Mediterranean flavors, with the freshness of lemon and the richness of almonds. This cake is perfect for those following a keto-Mediterranean diet or wanting to reduce sugar and carb intake. The low-carb sweetener offers a delightful sweetness without compromising the taste. Serve the lemon and almond cake as a dessert after a meal or as a light snack. Enjoy every bite of this guilt-free delight and let yourself be captivated by the authentic flavors of the Mediterranean diet.

2.Dark Chocolate Mousse with Orange Zest

The Dark Chocolate Mousse with Orange Zest is an irresistible keto-Mediterranean dessert that combines the intense taste of dark chocolate with the freshness of citrus. This creamy and velvety mousse is enriched with the aromatic touch of orange zest, creating a perfect balance between sweetness and acidity. The Dark Chocolate Mousse with Orange Zest is a treat to savor, ideal for concluding a special dinner or for indulging in a delightful treat.

Ingredients:

- 200g of 70% cocoa dark chocolate, broken into pieces
- 1 cup of fresh cream (sugar-free)
- 3 egg yolks
- Zest of 1 untreated orange
- 2 tablespoons of erythritol (or another low-carb sweetener)
- 1 teaspoon of vanilla extract

Preparation:

1. In a heat-resistant bowl, place the broken dark chocolate.

2. In a saucepan, heat the fresh cream over medium-high heat until it starts to boil.

3. Pour the boiling cream over the dark chocolate and mix until the chocolate is completely melted and the mixture is smooth and homogeneous.

4. Add the egg yolks to the melted chocolate mixture and mix quickly to combine the ingredients.

5. Add the grated orange zest, erythritol, and vanilla extract. Continue mixing until all ingredients are well incorporated.

6. Allow the mixture to cool slightly, then cover it with plastic wrap touching the surface of the mousse to prevent a skin from forming.

7. Place the mousse in the refrigerator and let it cool completely for at least 2-3 hours, or until it has reached the desired consistency.

8. Once the mousse is thoroughly chilled, serve it in dessert bowls.

9. Garnish with some grated orange zest before serving.

The Dark Chocolate Mousse with Orange Zest is a true delight for chocolate and citrus lovers. The combination of dark chocolate with the freshness of orange zest creates a velvety and flavorful mousse with a light citrus note. This mousse is sugar-free and pairs perfectly with a keto-Mediterranean diet. Serve it as a dessert after a special dinner or as a treat to conclude a meal in style. Delight your guests with this treat and let yourself be won over by the authentic flavors of the Mediterranean diet.

3.Vanilla Panna Cotta with Raspberry Coulis

The Vanilla Panna Cotta with Raspberry Coulis is a keto-Mediterranean dessert that will delight the palate with its creaminess and the delicate flavor of vanilla, enriched by the fruity and tangy taste of raspberry coulis. This delicacy offers a combination of flavors that harmoniously blend, creating a refined and irresistible dessert. The panna cotta is sweetened with a low-carb sweetener, making it perfect for those following a keto-Mediterranean diet or wanting to reduce sugar intake.

Ingredients:

- 2 cups of fresh cream (sugar-free)
- 1/4 cup of erythritol (or another low-carb sweetener)
- 1 vanilla bean (or 1 teaspoon of vanilla extract)
- 4 gelatin sheets
- 1 cup of fresh or frozen raspberries
- 1 tablespoon of erythritol (or another low-carb sweetener)
- Juice of half a lemon

Preparation:

1. In a pot, warm the fresh cream over medium heat. Add the erythritol and vanilla bean (or vanilla extract) and stir well until the sweetener has dissolved.

2. Remove the pot from the heat and let it infuse for 10-15 minutes so the vanilla releases its aroma into the cream.

3. Meanwhile, place the gelatin sheets in cold water and let them soften for about 5 minutes.

4. Slightly reheat the vanilla cream, then squeeze out the softened gelatin sheets to remove excess water and add them to the cream. Stir well until the gelatin is completely dissolved.

5. Pour the panna cotta into molds or dessert cups and let it cool to room temperature for a few minutes.

6. Place the panna cotta in the refrigerator and let it cool and solidify for at least 3-4 hours, or better if overnight.

7. To prepare the raspberry coulis, place the raspberries and erythritol in a small pot over medium heat. Add the lemon juice and cook the

raspberries until they become soft and release their juice.

8. Blend the cooked raspberries until smooth and strain the coulis to remove seeds.

9. Allow the raspberry coulis to cool to room temperature.

10. Once the panna cotta is cold and solidified, serve each cup with a generous spoonful of raspberry coulis on top.

The Vanilla Panna Cotta with Raspberry Coulis is a dessert that enchants with its delicacy and balance of flavors. The creamy panna cotta, sweetened with a low-carb sweetener, pairs wonderfully with the freshness and acidity of the raspberry coulis. Vanilla adds an aromatic and refined touch to the panna cotta, while the raspberry coulis provides a fruity and vibrant note. Serve this delicacy after a special dinner or to conclude a meal in a sophisticated manner. Let yourself be seduced by the authentic flavors of the Mediterranean diet and savor every spoonful of this keto-Mediterranean delight.

4.Chocolate and Avocado Cheesecake

The Chocolate and Avocado Cheesecake is an irresistible and healthy take on a classic dessert loved by all. This keto-Mediterranean version combines the creaminess of fresh cheese and avocado with the bold taste of dark chocolate. The crunchy base of nuts and chocolate completes the dessert, creating a combination of flavors and textures that will satisfy your sweet cravings without compromising your diet. Prepare this cheesecake for a special dinner or a sweet snack with friends and family.

Ingredients for the base:

- 1 cup of nuts
- 1/4 cup of unsweetened cocoa powder
- 2 tablespoons of erythritol (or another low-carb sweetener)
- 2 tablespoons of unsalted butter, melted

Ingredients for the cream:

- 2 ripe avocados, peeled and pitted
- 250 g of spreadable fresh cheese (like Philadelphia), at room temperature
- 1/2 cup of unsweetened cocoa powder
- 1/2 cup of erythritol (or another low-carb sweetener)
- 1 teaspoon of vanilla extract
- A pinch of salt
- Dark chocolate shavings for garnishing (optional)

Preparation:

1. Preheat the oven to 180°C (350°F) and prepare a 20 cm springform pan by lining it with parchment paper.

2. In a blender, finely grind the nuts with the cocoa powder and erythritol until it reaches a breadcrumb-like consistency.

3. Add the melted butter to the nut and cocoa mixture and mix well until you achieve a sandy consistency.

4. Pour the nut and cocoa base into the prepared mold and press firmly with the back of a spoon to compact it evenly at the bottom of the mold.

5. Bake the nut base in the preheated oven for about 10 minutes, then remove from the oven and let it cool completely.

6. In a blender, blend the ripe avocados until you get a smooth and lump-free cream.

7. Add the spreadable fresh cheese, cocoa powder, erythritol, vanilla extract, and a pinch of salt to the blended avocados.

8. Blend all the ingredients together until you get a smooth and velvety cream.

9. Pour the chocolate and avocado cream over the cooled nut base and level it with a spatula.

10. Place the cheesecake in the refrigerator and let it cool and solidify for at least 4-6 hours, or better if overnight.

11. Before serving, garnish the cheesecake with dark chocolate shavings, if desired.

The Chocolate and Avocado Cheesecake is a delicious and healthy version of a classic cheesecake. The creaminess of the avocado combines with the spreadable fresh cheese and the intense flavor of dark chocolate, creating a velvety and tasty mousse. The base of nuts and cocoa provides a crunchy and nutritious note to the dessert. This cheesecake is sugar-free and suitable for a keto-Mediterranean diet. Serve it as a dessert to conclude a special meal or to pamper yourself with a scrumptious and balanced treat. Delight your guests with this delicacy and let yourself be captivated by the authentic flavors of the Mediterranean diet.

5. Pistachio Ice Cream Without Sugar

Pistachio Ice Cream Without Sugar is a sweet and creamy keto-Mediterranean dessert that delights the senses with the rich and nutritious taste of pistachios, without the addition of refined sugar. This homemade ice cream offers a healthy and tasty alternative to traditional ice creams, thanks to the use of low-carb sweeteners. The richness of the pistachios blends harmoniously with the freshness of the ice cream, giving you an authentic and satisfying taste experience.

Ingredients:

- 2 cups of fresh cream (sugar-free)
- 1 cup of unsweetened almond milk
- 1/2 cup of erythritol (or another low-carb sweetener)
- 1 cup of unsalted shelled pistachios
- 1 teaspoon of vanilla extract

Preparation:

1. In a mixer, finely chop the shelled pistachios until you get a pistachio powder. You can leave some whole to set aside for decorating the ice cream at the end.

2. In a bowl, mix the fresh cream, almond milk, erythritol, vanilla extract, and pistachio powder. Make sure the sweetener is completely dissolved.

3. Pour the ice cream mixture into the ice cream maker and start the freezing process according to the instructions of your machine.

4. If you do not have an ice cream maker, pour the ice cream mixture into a shallow container and put it in the freezer. Every 30-40 minutes, stir the ice cream with a fork to break up the ice crystals and obtain a creamier consistency. Continue to repeat this operation until the ice cream is completely frozen and creamy.

5. Transfer the pistachio ice cream to a sealable container and put it in the freezer for at least 2-3 hours or until it reaches the desired consistency.

6. Before serving, leave the pistachio ice cream at room temperature for a few minutes to soften slightly.

7. If desired, garnish the pistachio ice cream with some whole pistachios before serving.

Pistachio Ice Cream Without Sugar is an explosion of taste for pistachio lovers. The creaminess and richness of the pistachios blend with the freshness of the ice cream, creating a delicacy that will satisfy your sweet tooth without compromising your keto-Mediterranean diet. Enjoy Pistachio Ice Cream Without Sugar as a dessert after a meal or as a delicious snack on a warm summer day. Let yourself be conquered by the authentic flavors of the Mediterranean diet and enjoy every spoonful of this healthy delight.

6.White Chocolate Mousse Cups with Red Berries

White Chocolate Mousse Cups with Red Berries are an elegant and delicious combination of flavors that combines the delicate sweetness of white chocolate with the freshness and acidity of red berries. This velvety mousse, enriched with berries such as strawberries, raspberries, and blueberries, offers an irresistible taste experience. The sweetness is balanced by using low-carb sweeteners, making this delicacy perfect for a keto-Mediterranean diet. Prepare these mousse cups for a special dinner or to conclude a meal in style and enjoy every bite of this refined delight.

Ingredients for the mousse:

- 200 g of sugar-free white chocolate, broken into pieces
- 1 cup of fresh cream (sugar-free)
- 1/2 cup of unsweetened almond milk
- 2 egg yolks
- 2 tablespoons of erythritol (or another low-carb sweetener)
- 1 teaspoon of vanilla extract

Ingredients for the red berry sauce:

- 1 cup of mixed red berries (strawberries, raspberries, blueberries)
- 1 tablespoon of erythritol (or another low-carb sweetener)
- Juice of half a lemon

Preparation:

1. In a saucepan, heat the fresh cream and almond milk over medium-low heat until it starts to boil.
2. In a bowl, beat the egg yolks with erythritol until smooth.
3. Slowly pour the hot cream and milk into the bowl with the beaten egg yolks, stirring constantly to avoid cooking the yolks.
4. Transfer the egg and cream mixture back into the saucepan and cook over medium-low heat, stirring constantly with a spatula, until the mixture thickens slightly and coats the back of the spatula.
5. Remove the saucepan from the heat and add the broken white chocolate, stirring well until the chocolate is completely melted.

6. Add the vanilla extract to the mixture and stir until you get a smooth and velvety mousse.

7. Pour the white chocolate mousse into cups or dessert glasses and let cool at room temperature for a few minutes.

8. Put the mousse cups in the refrigerator and let them cool and solidify for at least 2-3 hours, or better if overnight.

9. In the meantime, prepare the red berry sauce: in a blender, blend the red berries with erythritol and lemon juice until you get a smooth and homogeneous sauce.

10. Before serving, pour the red berry sauce over the white chocolate mousse in the cups.

White Chocolate Mousse Cups with Red Berries are an elegant and delicious delicacy that combines white chocolate with the freshness and acidity of red berries. The white chocolate mousse is creamy and velvety, while the red berry sauce provides a fruity and juicy note to the dessert. This delicacy is sugar-free and suitable for a keto-Mediterranean diet. Serve the mousse cups as a dessert to conclude a special dinner or to pamper yourself with a refined treat. Delight your guests with this delicacy and let yourself be conquered by the authentic flavors of the Mediterranean diet.

7. Berry Tart with Walnut Crust

The Berry Tart with Walnut Crust is an irresistible keto-Mediterranean dessert that celebrates the flavors and colors of berries in a tart with a crunchy and nutritious walnut base. This tart is free from sugar and refined flours but is rich in taste and nutrients. The natural sweetness of the berries and the use of low-carb sweeteners make this tart perfect for those following a keto-Mediterranean diet or wanting to reduce sugar intake. Prepare this tart for a special occasion or indulge yourself with a delicious and healthy dessert.

Ingredients for the base:

- 1 cup of walnuts
- 2 tablespoons of erythritol (or another low-carb sweetener)
- 3 tablespoons of unsalted butter, melted

Ingredients for the filling:

- 2 cups of mixed berries (strawberries, raspberries, blueberries, blackberries, etc.)
- 2 tablespoons of erythritol (or another low-carb sweetener)
- 1 tablespoon of cornstarch or coconut flour (to thicken the filling)

Preparation:

1. Preheat the oven to 180°C (350°F) and prepare a tart mold, lining it with parchment paper or greasing it with butter and walnut flour.

2. In a blender, finely chop the walnuts until you get a fine flour.

3. In a bowl, mix the walnut flour, erythritol, and melted butter until you get a sandy dough.

4. Pour the walnut mixture into the tart mold and press it well with your hands to form an even base on the bottom and sides of the mold.

5. Bake the walnut base in a preheated oven for about 10-12 minutes, or until it turns golden. Keep an eye on the cooking to prevent the crust from burning.

6. While the walnut base cools slightly, prepare the filling. In a bowl, mix the berries with the erythritol and cornstarch or coconut flour until the fruits are evenly coated.

7. Pour the berry filling onto the preheated walnut base and level it with a spatula.

8. Put the berry tart back in the oven and bake for another 20-25 minutes, or until the filling becomes soft and juicy.

9. Remove the tart from the oven and let it cool completely before serving.

The Berry Tart with Walnut Crust is an explosion of colors and flavors that will delight you. The crunchy and nutritious walnut base provides a perfect contrast to the juicy sweetness of the berries. This tart is sugar-free and suitable for a keto-Mediterranean diet. Serve it as a dessert to end a special dinner or pamper yourself with a delicious and healthy treat. Let yourself be captivated by the authentic flavors of the Mediterranean diet and enjoy every slice of this delicacy.

8. Almond and Cocoa Tiramisu Without Sugar

The Almond and Cocoa Tiramisu Without Sugar is a refined and keto-Mediterranean version of the famous Italian dessert. This delicacy replaces the traditional mascarpone with an almond cream and uses unsweetened cocoa powder to give a delicate chocolate aroma. Without the addition of refined sugar, this tiramisu is sweetened with a low-carb sweetener, making it suitable for a keto-Mediterranean diet. Prepare this tasty variant of tiramisu to conclude a special dinner or indulge yourself with a delicious and healthy dessert.

Ingredients for the almond cream:

- 1 cup of raw almonds, peeled and soaked in water for at least 4 hours
- 1/4 cup of fresh cream (sugar-free)
- 2 tablespoons of erythritol (or other low-carb sweetener)
- 1 teaspoon of vanilla extract
- 1 pinch of salt

Ingredients for assembling the tiramisu:

- 16-20 sugar-free ladyfingers (adjustable to the size of your mold)
- 1 cup of cooled coffee
- 2 tablespoons of unsweetened cocoa powder for garnishing

Preparation:

1. In a blender, blend the drained and softened almonds with the fresh cream, erythritol, vanilla extract, and salt until you get a smooth and homogeneous cream.
2. Make sure to drain the almonds well before blending to get a creamy consistency without excess liquid.
3. Transfer the almond cream to a bowl and refrigerate for at least 30 minutes to cool and thicken slightly.
4. Meanwhile, prepare the coffee and let it cool completely.
5. Prepare your tiramisu mold, adjusting its size to the sugar-free ladyfingers you will use.

6. Quickly dip the cooled ladyfingers into the coffee and arrange them at the bottom of the mold.

7. Cover the biscuits with a layer of almond cream and level it with a spatula.

8. Continue to make alternating layers of coffee-soaked ladyfingers and almond cream until you run out of ingredients.

9. The last layer should be almond cream.

10. Cover the mold with plastic wrap and refrigerate the tiramisu for at least 4 hours or, better, overnight, to flavor the biscuits well and thicken the cream.

11. Before serving, sprinkle the tiramisu with unsweetened cocoa powder.

The Almond and Cocoa Tiramisu Without Sugar is an elegant variant of the classic tiramisu, offering a combination of delicate and irresistible flavors. The almond cream gives a creamy and enveloping note, while the unsweetened cocoa powder provides a subtle chocolate aroma. Without the addition of refined sugar, this tiramisu is suitable for a keto-Mediterranean diet, satisfying your craving for sweetness without guilt. Serve this delicious dessert after a special meal or to end a dinner with style. Let yourself be captivated by the authentic flavors of the Mediterranean diet and enjoy every spoonful of this delicacy.

9.Vanilla Chia Pudding with Red Berries

Vanilla Chia Pudding with Red Berries is a fresh and nutritious dessert that combines the sweetness of vanilla with the gelatinous consistency and nutrient-rich chia seeds. The delicious vanilla cream merges with the tartness of red fruits such as strawberries, raspberries, and blueberries, creating an irresistible flavor balance. This pudding is sugar-free and suitable for a keto-Mediterranean diet. Prepare this delicacy for a healthy snack or as a light dessert after a meal.

Ingredients for vanilla pudding:

- 1 cup unsweetened almond milk
- 1/4 cup chia seeds
- 2 tablespoons erythritol (or another low-carb sweetener)
- 1 teaspoon vanilla extract

Ingredients for red berry sauce:

- 1 cup mixed red berries (strawberries, raspberries, blueberries)
- 1 tablespoon erythritol (or another low-carb sweetener)
- Juice of half a lemon

Preparation:

1. In a bowl, mix almond milk, chia seeds, erythritol, and vanilla extract. Ensure the sweetener is fully dissolved.
2. Cover the bowl with cling film and refrigerate for at least 2 hours, or preferably overnight, to let the pudding set.
3. Meanwhile, prepare the red berry sauce: in a blender, blend red berries with erythritol and lemon juice until smooth.
4. Once the vanilla chia pudding reaches the desired consistency, fill dessert cups or glasses halfway.
5. Pour some red berry sauce over the pudding.
6. Add another layer of vanilla chia pudding over the red berry sauce.
7. Continue layering pudding and sauce until you run out of ingredients.
8. The top layer should be red berry sauce.
9. Garnish with some fresh red berries before serving.

Enjoy the refreshing and nutritious Vanilla Chia Pudding with Red Berries without any guilt. The gelatinous texture of chia seeds pairs with the delicious vanilla cream, while the tartness and freshness of the red berries add a fruity touch to the dessert. Perfect for a keto-Mediterranean diet, this balanced and healthy dessert will satiate your sweet cravings. Enjoy every spoonful of this delicacy, representing the authentic flavors of the Mediterranean diet.

10.Cream Ice Cream with Stevia Caramel and Walnuts

Cream Ice Cream with Stevia Caramel and Walnuts is a soft and velvety dessert that offers the indulgent taste of cream ice cream without any guilt. This creamy ice cream is sweetened with stevia caramel, providing natural sweetness without added sugar. Crunchy walnuts enrich the ice cream, adding a crispy and nutritious touch. Perfect for a keto-Mediterranean diet or for those looking to reduce sugar intake. Prepare this ice cream to refresh yourself on hot summer days or to indulge in a delicious and healthy treat.

Ingredients for the cream ice cream:

- 2 cups of fresh cream (unsweetened)
- 1 cup unsweetened almond milk
- 4 egg yolks
- 1/2 cup stevia caramel (prepared as per product instructions)
- 1 teaspoon vanilla extract

Ingredients for caramelized walnuts:

- 1 cup walnuts
- 2 tablespoons stevia caramel

Preparation:

1. In a bowl, whisk the egg yolks until smooth.

2. In a saucepan, heat the fresh cream and almond milk over medium-low heat until they begin to boil.

3. Slowly pour the hot cream and milk mixture into the bowl with the whisked yolks, continuously stirring to prevent the yolks from cooking.

4. Return the mixture to the saucepan and cook over medium-low heat, stirring constantly until it slightly thickens and coats the back of a spatula.

5. Remove from heat and mix in the stevia caramel and vanilla extract until smooth.

6. Allow the cream ice cream to cool to room temperature and then refrigerate for at least 2-3 hours, or preferably overnight, for a perfect consistency.

7. Meanwhile, prepare the caramelized walnuts: toast the walnuts in a non-stick pan over medium heat until fragrant.

8. Add the stevia caramel to the toasted walnuts, mixing well.

9. Transfer the caramelized walnuts to parchment paper and let them cool.

10. When the cream ice cream reaches the desired consistency, pour it into an ice cream maker and follow your machine's instructions.

11. If you don't have an ice cream maker, pour the cream ice cream into a shallow container and freeze. Every 30-40 minutes, stir the ice cream with a fork to break up the ice crystals and achieve a creamier consistency. Repeat this process until the ice cream is fully frozen and creamy.

12. Garnish with caramelized walnuts before serving.

Indulge in the rich and healthy Cream Ice Cream with Stevia Caramel and Walnuts, satisfying your ice cream cravings without affecting your keto-Mediterranean diet. The creaminess of the ice cream harmoniously blends with the sweetness of the stevia caramel, while the caramelized walnuts add a crispy and nutritious touch. Enjoy this treat on hot summer days or as a dessert after a meal. Relish the authentic flavors of the Mediterranean diet with every spoonful of this wholesome delight. Bon appétit!

CHAPTER 9: Facing Challenges: How to Handle Common Obstacles and Initial Symptoms

One of the first challenges encountered when starting a ketogenic diet is the body's adaptation to a new type of metabolism. Normally, the body uses carbohydrates as its primary energy source. However, when following a ketogenic diet, carbohydrate intake is limited, forcing the body to use fats as its main energy source.

This process is known as ketosis, and it is the primary goal of the keto diet. During the adaptation phase to the ketogenic metabolism, it's common to experience a range of symptoms often referred to as "keto flu." These can include headaches, fatigue, brain fog, irritability, constipation, muscle cramps, and concentration difficulties.

Despite its name, the keto flu isn't an actual flu but rather a series of symptoms resulting from the body adapting to the new metabolism.

Here are some ways to handle the keto flu and ease the transition to a ketogenic metabolism:

Adequate Hydration: One of the most common symptoms of keto flu is dehydration.

This can be caused by an increase in urination due to reduced carbohydrate intake. Ensuring you drink plenty of water throughout the day can help prevent dehydration and reduce related symptoms.

Mineral Intake: The increased urination can also lead to a loss of electrolytes like sodium, potassium, and magnesium. Supplementing your diet with these minerals can help prevent muscle cramps and maintain electrolyte balance.

Gradual Transition: Instead of directly transitioning to a strict ketogenic diet, it might be helpful to start with a low-carbohydrate diet and gradually reduce carbohydrate intake over several weeks. This can help the body adapt to the new metabolism and lessen the intensity of keto flu symptoms.

The keto flu is temporary. As the body adjusts to ketosis, symptoms should decrease and eventually disappear. During this adjustment period, it's essential to listen to your body and take care of yourself.

If symptoms persist or become too challenging to handle, consulting a health professional to discuss potential dietary modifications or the adaptation plan might be beneficial.

Embarking on a new dietary lifestyle, like the keto-Mediterranean diet, can be challenging, especially when faced with temptations and social pressures.

Dining out with friends, parties, birthdays, or merely the desire for a non-keto treat can seem insurmountable obstacles.

It's essential to remember that the keto-Mediterranean diet isn't just a dietary regimen, but a life choice aimed at improving long-term health and well-being. Here are some practical tips for managing these situations:

Planning: Before attending social events, plan. If possible, find out which foods will be served and plan accordingly. If the menu doesn't suit your new dietary style, eat something at home before the event or bring a keto-Mediterranean meal with you. In many restaurants, it's possible to request modifications to dishes to make them more keto-friendly.

Communication: Don't hesitate to share your choice of following a keto-Mediterranean diet. Those around you might not be aware of your dietary choices and might unintentionally offer you foods incompatible with your diet. Making your dietary needs known can help prevent awkward situations and allow friends and family to support you.

Flexibility: Remember, following a keto-Mediterranean diet doesn't mean you must completely forgo your favorite foods. Many keto-friendly recipes replicate favorite dishes using low-carb ingredients.

Moreover, occasionally indulging in a treat or a non-keto meal won't derail your progress, provided you promptly return to your keto-Mediterranean plan.

Support: Seek support from individuals who share your journey or back your choices. Join online support groups, follow blogs, or social media accounts dedicated to the keto-Mediterranean diet. Having a support network can make a significant difference in your journey.

Facing temptations and social pressures can be challenging, but with the right mindset and some practical strategies, you can navigate these situations successfully and maintain your keto-Mediterranean diet. Remember, every small step you take toward a healthier lifestyle is a success.

Physical exercise plays a crucial role in achieving holistic well-being and maximizing the results of the keto-Mediterranean diet. Navigating through the changes associated with physical activity on this diet might require a different approach than usual.

Firstly, it's vital to pay attention to how your body feels during exercise, especially at the beginning of the diet. During the adaptation period, a temporary decrease in energy or performance might occur. This is a standard aspect of the body transitioning to ketosis.

In the meantime, engaging in lower-intensity exercises like walking, yoga, or gentle cycling could be a sensible choice.

Over time, the body will adapt to the new energy source, allowing for a gradual increase in workout intensity. An essential component of the exercise program should be the incorporation of exercises promoting mobility and flexibility, ensuring muscle and joint health, and reducing the risk of potential injuries.

Managing water and electrolyte balance is another aspect that deserves attention. Physical activity, combined with the keto diet, can accelerate electrolyte loss through sweat. Ensure an adequate intake of electrolytes, especially sodium, potassium, and magnesium.

This can be achieved through dietary sources or supplements. Consider hydrating with electrolyte-rich drinks before and after exercises. Finally, remember that physical activity is not just about structured workouts.

Integrating daily movement into your routine, like taking stairs instead of elevators or parking further away, can help burn extra calories and enhance overall well-being.

Incorporating regular exercise into your routine, combined with the keto-Mediterranean diet, can pave the way for optimal health and longevity.

Remember to listen to your body, adjust as needed, and embrace physical activity as an essential aspect of your new lifestyle.

Diving deeper into various types of exercise, each has a distinct role to play in optimizing your keto-Mediterranean journey.

Understanding how each of these exercises interacts with your body and diet is crucial for maximizing benefits. While resistance exercise may immediately appear tied to muscle building, its link with the keto-Mediterranean diet is profound.

This high-fat, protein-rich diet provides the energy required for workout sessions while supporting post-workout muscle growth and repair. Therefore, resistance exercise becomes a key component of this synergy, as it not only helps develop more muscle mass which in turn burns more calories but also promotes a more efficient use of ingested nutrients.

Cardiovascular exercise, or cardio, is another key player. Although the keto-Mediterranean diet is low in carbohydrates, the energy needed for aerobic activities comes from fat sources, abundant in this dietary regime. Cardio training thus becomes an effective means to utilize these fats, contributing to sustainable weight loss and improved cardiovascular health.

Whether you choose to walk in the local park, cycle, or swim, cardio should be a fundamental component of your exercise regime. Incorporating flexibility exercises like yoga and stretching might seem of lesser importance in a weight loss context, but they are vital for overall well-being.

Not only do they improve mobility and prevent injuries, but they also help reduce stress and promote a positive mood. Moreover, the link between good mental health and effective weight loss is well-documented, making flexibility exercises an essential element for long-term success.

Integrating resistance, cardio, and flexibility exercises can provide a balanced workout program that enhances your keto-Mediterranean diet, improving body composition and overall health. The key is remembering there's no one-size-fits-all approach; finding the right balance between these exercises tailored to your personal needs, goals, and lifestyle will be the key to your success. In the intricate dance of diet and physical exercise, understanding how energy and performance can be optimized is crucial.

A keto-Mediterranean diet offers a unique approach to energy and performance, with its high share of fats and proteins providing a steady and enduring fuel source for physical activities.

Starting with the initial adaptation period, also known as "keto flu", this is a time when your body is getting accustomed to burning fats for energy instead of carbohydrates.

During this time, you may experience a temporary reduction in physical performance. Fear not, though, it's only temporary. As your body adjusts to the new diet and starts producing ketone bodies as its primary energy source, you'll see a return and, in many cases, an enhancement in your physical performance.

One of the main challenges you might face while exercising on a keto diet is maintaining energy levels. Unlike the high-carb diet where energy can drastically fluctuate based on blood sugar levels, the keto-Mediterranean diet provides a steady energy release due to its high fat content.

This can help you avoid energy dips during workouts and maintain consistent performance. The keto-Mediterranean diet can also help optimize your endurance.

Since your body utilizes fats as its primary energy source, you have access to an almost limitless fuel reserve. This is particularly useful for endurance or long-duration workouts, where your body's ability to use fats as fuel can give you an edge. But what about strength and power? Although carbs are often viewed as the preferred fuel for high-intensity workouts, research has shown a keto diet can effectively support these sessions. This is partly since, although your body adapts to burning fats, it will continue to preserve a certain amount of glycogen for high-intensity activities. After putting time and effort into effective training, it's essential to pay equal attention to post-workout recovery. Recovery is the period when the body rejuvenates and restores, preparing for the next workout.

Proper recovery is crucial for maximizing workout benefits, improving physical performance, and reducing the risk of injuries. Post-workout nutrition is a key component of recovery. This is when your body needs nutrients to repair muscles, restore energy, and foster adaptation to training.

But how does the keto-Mediterranean diet fit into this picture? In a keto-Mediterranean diet, the post-workout focus should be on foods rich in quality proteins and fats. Proteins are vital for repairing and building muscles, while fats help restore energy levels and support many of the body's vital functions. You might be surprised to learn that, unlike a traditional high-carb diet, a keto-Mediterranean diet doesn't necessitate a massive intake of carbohydrates post-workout.

Since your body adapts to use fats as its primary energy source, there's no need to "reload" glycogen stores with a carb-heavy meal. However, a small intake of carbohydrates from leafy greens or other low-carb sources can be beneficial, especially after particularly intense or long-duration workouts. An example of a keto-Mediterranean post-workout meal might include a serving of protein, such as chicken or fish, accompanied by leafy greens and dressed with extra-virgin olive oil. Including a small snack of nuts or seeds for additional protein and fats might also be beneficial.

Moreover, it's essential to remember that rehydration is a crucial aspect of recovery. Physical exercise can lead to significant fluid and electrolyte loss, especially on a keto diet where diuresis can be enhanced. Ensure you drink plenty of water post-workout and, if necessary, consider supplementing with electrolytes.

Post-workout recovery goes beyond mere nutrition. It's about giving your body the time and resources it needs to regenerate and grow. This includes quality sleep, stress management, and sometimes even a break from physical training.

Remember, it's during rest that the body heals and gets stronger. Overtraining, without adequate recovery, can lead to diminished results, increased risk of injuries, and chronic fatigue.

In conclusion, combining the keto-Mediterranean diet with a balanced exercise regimen can yield impressive results. By understanding the synergies between this diet and various exercise types, you can optimize your health, performance, and physique. Whether your goals are weight loss, muscle gain, or simply maintaining a healthy lifestyle, this combination can help pave the way for success.

CHAPTER 10 Physical Exercise and Keto-Mediterranean Diet: How to Optimize Results

Physical exercise is a fundamental element of any health and wellness plan, and the keto-Mediterranean diet is no exception. Physical activity, in tandem with optimal nutrition, can significantly enhance the desired results, whether it's weight loss, overall health improvement, or athletic performance enhancement.

The keto-Mediterranean diet, combining the principles of the Mediterranean diet and the carbohydrate restriction of the ketogenic diet, provides a nutritional framework that can be further enhanced through physical exercise. Physical activity not only helps burn more calories and improve body composition but is also a potent means to improve psychological well-being, reduce stress, and enhance sleep quality.

The core advantage of incorporating physical exercise into the keto-Mediterranean diet lies in its ability to boost metabolism. An efficient metabolism can facilitate the body's shift into a state of ketosis, a key goal of the keto diet, where the body uses fats as the primary energy source rather than carbohydrates.

Physical exercise can also help maintain muscles during a keto diet, a crucial aspect to prevent muscle loss, especially during weight loss.

Physical exercise can enhance overall health in many ways, regardless of whether one is following a keto-Mediterranean diet or not. It can reduce the risk of chronic diseases like heart diseases and type 2 diabetes, improve bone and joint health, and even aid in enhancing cognitive function and mood. It can be a powerful means to achieve and maintain a healthy weight, a key objective for many following the keto-Mediterranean diet. When combined with a keto-Mediterranean diet, physical exercise can help create a healthy caloric deficit, facilitating weight loss and aiding in long-term weight maintenance.

Overall, the incorporation of physical exercise into the keto-Mediterranean diet can lead to a host of benefits, enhancing health and well-being in ways that go beyond mere weight loss. As such, it's a component worth considering in the context of a comprehensive keto-Mediterranean diet plan.

After emphasizing the importance of physical exercise in tandem with the keto-Mediterranean diet, it's beneficial to understand which types of physical activities can be incorporated to optimize results.

The combination of resistance, cardio, and flexibility exercises can offer a balanced and sustainable approach to training.

Resistance exercises, also known as weight training, play a fundamental role. This kind of exercise is vital for maintaining and building muscle mass. Having more muscles can boost metabolism, allowing the body to burn more calories, even at rest. Resistance exercises include activities like weightlifting, push-ups, leg bends, and abdominal crunches. The key is to start slowing and gradually increase the intensity and volume to prevent injuries and ensure safe progression.

Cardio, or aerobic exercise, is another cornerstone of a physical exercise regimen. This type of exercise is effective for burning calories and improving cardiovascular health. Activities like walking, running, cycling, or swimming are all excellent options.

It's essential to note that the intensity of aerobic exercise should be tailored to individual capacities and should be increased gradually to avoid overtraining or injuries.

Flexibility exercises, such as stretching and yoga, might seem less critical for weight loss, but they are, in fact, vital for overall health and well-being. They enhance joint mobility, prevent injuries, and can even contribute to stress reduction and a positive mood.

Incorporating a few minutes of stretching or yoga into your daily routine can make a significant difference in the long run.

The combination of these three exercise types can provide a balanced workout program that promotes muscular, cardiovascular, and overall health. When integrated with the keto-Mediterranean diet, they can help optimize results by improving body composition, overall health, and well-being. Remember, every individual is unique, and the best exercise routine will be the one that caters to your personal needs, goals, and lifestyle.

Delving deeper into the various types of exercises, each has a distinct role in optimizing your keto-Mediterranean journey.

Understanding how each of these exercises interacts with your body and the diet is crucial to maximizing benefits.

While resistance exercise might seem directly tied to muscle building, its connection with the keto-Mediterranean diet runs deep. This high-fat, protein-rich diet provides the energy required for workout sessions while supporting post-exercise muscle growth and repair.

Consequently, resistance exercise becomes a key component of this synergy, as it not only helps develop greater muscle mass which in turn burns more calories, but it also promotes a more efficient use of consumed nutrients.

Cardiovascular exercise, or cardio, is another key player. Although the keto-Mediterranean diet is low in carbs, the energy required for aerobic activities comes from fat sources, abundant in this diet. Cardio training can thus become an effective means to utilize these fats, contributing to sustainable weight loss and improved cardiovascular health.

Whether you decide to walk in the local park, cycle, or swim, cardio should be a fundamental component of your exercise program.

The incorporation of flexibility exercises, like yoga and stretching, might seem of lesser importance in a weight loss context, but these are vital for maintaining overall well-being. They not only enhance mobility and prevent injuries but also help reduce stress and foster a positive mood. Furthermore, the link between good mental health and effective weight loss is well-documented, making flexibility exercises an essential element for long-term success.

Integrating resistance, cardio, and flexibility exercises can provide a balanced workout regimen that enhances your keto-Mediterranean diet, improving body composition and overall health. The key is to remember that there isn't a one-size-fits-all approach; finding the right balance among these exercises that caters to your personal needs, goals, and lifestyle will be the key to your success.

In the intricate dance of diet and exercise, understanding how energy and performance can be optimized is crucial. A keto-Mediterranean diet offers a unique approach to energy and performance, with its high fat and protein content providing a steady and long-lasting fuel source for physical activities.

Let's start with the initial adaptation period, also known as the "keto flu". This is a time when your body is getting used to burning fat for energy instead of carbohydrates. During this time, you may experience a temporary decrease in physical performance. Fear not, though, this is only temporary. As your body gets used to the new diet and starts producing ketone bodies as the primary energy source, you'll see a return and, in many cases, an enhancement of your physical performance.

One of the main challenges you may face during physical exercise on a keto diet is maintaining energy levels. Unlike high-carb diets, where energy can drastically fluctuate depending on blood sugar levels, the keto-Mediterranean diet provides a steady release of energy due to its high-fat content. This can help you avoid energy drops during training and maintain consistent performance.

The keto-Mediterranean diet can also help optimize your endurance. Since your body uses fats as the primary energy source, you have access to an almost unlimited fuel reserve. This is especially useful for endurance or long-duration workouts, where your body's ability to use fats as fuel can give you an edge.

But what about strength and power? Although carbohydrates are often seen as the preferred fuel for high-intensity workouts, research has shown that a keto diet can effectively support these sessions. This is partly since while your body adapts to burn fat, it will still retain some glycogen for high-intensity activities.

After dedicating time and energy to effective training, post-workout recovery is paramount. Recovery is the time when the body regenerates and restores, preparing for the next workout.

Proper recovery is vital to maximize training benefits, improve physical performance, and reduce injury risk.

Post-workout nutrition is a key component of recovery. This is when your body needs nutrients to repair muscles, restore energy, and foster training adaptation. But how does the keto-Mediterranean diet fit into this?

On a keto-Mediterranean diet, post-workout focus should be on foods rich in protein and quality fats. Proteins are essential for repairing and building muscles, while fats help restore energy levels and support many vital body functions.

You might be surprised to know that, unlike a traditional high-carb diet, a keto-Mediterranean diet doesn't require a massive intake of carbohydrates after exercise. Since your body adapts to using fats as its primary energy source, there's no need to "recharge" glycogen stores with a carb-rich meal. However, a small intake of carbohydrates from leafy greens or other low-carb sources can be beneficial, especially after particularly intense or long-duration workouts.

An example of a keto-Mediterranean post-workout meal might include a protein portion, such as chicken or fish, accompanied by leafy greens, and drizzled with extra-virgin olive oil.

Including a small snack of nuts or seeds for additional protein and fat intake might be helpful as well.

Additionally, it's important to remember that rehydration is a crucial aspect of recovery. Exercise can lead to significant fluid and electrolyte loss, especially on a keto diet where diuresis can be increased. Ensure you drink plenty of water post-exercise, and if needed, consider electrolyte supplementation.

Post-workout recovery goes beyond mere nutrition. It's about giving the body the time and resources it needs to regenerate and grow. This includes quality sleep, relaxation techniques like stretching or meditation, and of course, adequate nutrition. With proper attention to recovery, the keto-Mediterranean diet can not only support your training but also enhance your overall well-being.

Creating a personalized exercise program is the final piece in an optimal health journey combined with the keto-Mediterranean diet.

An effective strategy should align with your lifestyle, your goals, and your health status. A personalized program can boost your motivation, enhance your results, and make training a pleasurable and rewarding experience.

Personalization starts with understanding your preferences and goals. Do you enjoy high-intensity training, or do you prefer an outdoor walk? Are you aiming to build muscle mass, or is your main goal to improve your cardiovascular endurance? Gathering this information is the first step in creating a program that will motivate you to stay consistent.

Next, consider your physical abilities and health status. If you have health concerns or physical limitations, consulting a fitness professional or physician before starting a new training program might be beneficial. They can help tailor a program that's safe and effective for you.

Once you've identified your preferences and goals, it's time to structure your training program. A balanced mix of cardio, strength, and flexibility, as discussed in previous chapters, can offer a comprehensive approach to fitness. Each component can be tailored according to your needs. For instance, if your primary goal is muscle building, you might focus more on strength training but shouldn't neglect the importance of cardio and flexibility.

Your training program should be flexible and allow for changes. Your life is ever-evolving, and so should your training regimen.

Regularly evaluate your progress and adjust your program accordingly. You might discover a new type of exercise you love, or your goals might shift over time.

Remember that rest and recovery are fundamental parts of your training program. Allowing your body time to rest and regenerate is just as important as the training itself. Incorporate rest days into your routine and ensure you focus on post-workout nutrition and quality sleep.

Creating a personalized training program might seem daunting, but it's an investment in your long-term well-being.

With proper planning and attention, training can become an enjoyable and rewarding part of your keto-Mediterranean lifestyle. Remember, success isn't just measured by numbers on the scale or clothing size but by how you feel, your energy, and your zest for life.

CHAPTER 11 Long-Term Benefits: Heart Health, Weight Loss, and Beyond

The incidence of cardiovascular diseases is a growing concern worldwide, with numerous research efforts aiming to identify the most effective dietary strategies to prevent and manage these conditions. The keto-Mediterranean diet, in its remarkable union of two effective dietary approaches, has emerged as a potentially influential solution for optimizing cardiovascular health.

The keto-Mediterranean diet may have a beneficial effect on cholesterol levels. Diets rich in healthy fats, such as olive oil and fats from high-quality protein sources like fish, can help improve the ratio between LDL cholesterol, often termed "bad cholesterol", and HDL cholesterol, or "good cholesterol". Maintaining an optimal balance between these two types of cholesterol is crucial for preventing plaque buildup in the arteries and promoting healthy blood circulation, key elements in preventing cardiovascular diseases.

Similarly, the keto-Mediterranean diet can assist in better managing blood pressure.

Foods like leafy greens, rich in potassium, and fish, abundant in omega-3s, can help lower blood pressure. The abundance of such foods in this diet, combined with the absence of processed and high-salt foods, can support effective blood pressure regulation.

This diet has a direct protective effect on the heart. The high consumption of fruits and vegetables provides a large amount of antioxidants, compounds that help combat inflammation and protect cells from damage. This, coupled with the effect of healthy fats on cholesterol and blood pressure management, contributes to promoting heart health.

This diet can be a powerful ally for cardiovascular health. The beneficial effects of this diet on cholesterol regulation, blood pressure, and heart health may represent a significant step forward in preventing cardiovascular diseases and promoting a longer, healthier life.

Heart health is often linked to cholesterol levels in the blood, especially the ratio between "bad" LDL cholesterol and "good" HDL cholesterol. These two cholesterol types play different roles in the body: LDL tends to accumulate on artery walls, while HDL helps remove LDL from the system, thus reducing the risk of cardiovascular diseases.

The keto-Mediterranean diet, with its unique combination of foods, can positively influence the lipid profile, helping to manage cholesterol levels.

The keto-Mediterranean diet emphasizes the intake of healthy fats, such as those from olive oil and fish. These foods are rich in monounsaturated and polyunsaturated fatty acids, which have been linked to lower LDL cholesterol levels and higher HDL cholesterol levels. Moreover, olive oil, a staple of the Mediterranean diet, contains polyphenols, natural compounds proven to improve the lipid profile.

Another critical component is limiting carbohydrate intake, especially refined and high-glycemic index carbs. Studies have shown that a low-carb diet can reduce triglyceride levels, a type of blood fat that, when elevated, can increase cardiovascular disease risk. Limiting carb intake can also raise HDL levels.

Thus, combining the best of two healthy dietary approaches can help manage cholesterol levels. Consuming healthy fats, limiting refined and high-glycemic index carbs, together with incorporating antioxidant and fiber-rich foods, can help reduce LDL cholesterol and raise HDL, promoting a healthier lipid profile and better cardiovascular health.

Blood pressure, indicating the force with which blood pushes against artery walls, plays a vital role in heart health. High blood pressure values, or hypertension, can strain the heart and increase the risk of cardiovascular diseases. This is where the keto-Mediterranean diet comes into play: this dietary regimen offers numerous tools for managing and potentially reducing blood pressure.

A core feature of the keto-Mediterranean diet is the emphasis on whole foods, rich in fiber. High-fiber foods, like fruits, vegetables, and legumes, help lower blood pressure. Not only do they provide a feeling of fullness, preventing overeating and subsequent weight gain, but they also enhance gut health, a factor that can impact blood pressure.

Another component is the intake of healthy fats, particularly monounsaturated and polyunsaturated fatty acids. These fats, abundant in foods like olive oil, fish, and nuts, have been linked to lower blood pressure levels. Olive oil, in particular, has been associated with numerous heart health benefits, including blood pressure reduction.

Similarly, it encourages salt limitation, known to raise blood pressure.

Replacing salt with herbs and spices not only reduces sodium intake but also adds a flavor burst to dishes.

Together, these elements can contribute to healthy blood pressure. Adopting this diet, along with other lifestyle interventions like regular physical activity and stress management, can offer a powerful and natural way to optimize blood pressure and heart health.

Heart health is of vital importance since cardiovascular diseases remain among the leading global death causes. In this light, the keto-Mediterranean diet emerges as a potent ally in preventing and managing these diseases, thanks to its unique nutritional principles.

One of the key elements for heart health in this diet is the emphasis on healthy fats. The presence of monounsaturated and polyunsaturated fatty acids, like those found in olive oil, fish, and nuts, helps lower "bad" LDL cholesterol, and raise "good" HDL cholesterol. This cholesterol balance is crucial for preventing plaque accumulation in arteries, a condition leading to cardiovascular diseases like heart attacks.

Additionally, the high dietary fiber content from fruits, vegetables, and whole grains helps regulate blood pressure and maintain a healthy body weight, further critical factors for heart health.

This diet emphasizes the importance of moderate protein intake, primarily from lean sources like fish and poultry. This moderate protein intake, coupled with limited carbohydrate consumption, helps prevent systemic inflammation, a key risk factor for cardiovascular diseases.

These nutritional principles constitute a diet that can promote optimal heart health. By combining the keto-Mediterranean diet with other healthy lifestyle habits, such as regular exercise, stress management, and quality sleep, one can achieve a holistic approach to heart health. As always, it's important to remember that dietary changes should be undertaken in consultation with a health professional to ensure they meet individual needs and health goals.

Despite the significance of anecdotal evidence and individual experience playing a major role in shaping our perception of a particular diet, it's crucial to analyze what scientific research has to say about it. The keto-Mediterranean diet, like many other dietary strategies, has been the subject of numerous studies aimed at understanding its effects and potential health benefits.

Regarding cardiovascular benefits, several studies have highlighted the effectiveness of the keto-Mediterranean diet in promoting a healthier lipid profile.

For instance, a 2019 investigation published in a renowned English journal well-versed in the field showed a significant reduction in LDL levels (the so-called "bad cholesterol") in participants who followed a keto-Mediterranean diet. Similarly, an increase in HDL ("good") cholesterol was observed, key elements for the prevention of cardiovascular diseases.

Research has highlighted the potential of this diet in contributing to blood pressure regulation. An example is a 2017 study published in a renowned English journal, which showed a significant decrease in both systolic and diastolic blood pressure in subjects who followed a keto-Mediterranean diet.

Several longitudinal studies have confirmed that adherence to a Mediterranean dietary regimen, combined with the ketogenic approach, is associated with a reduced risk of cardiovascular diseases throughout life. A notable example is the PREDIMED study, a randomized clinical trial that demonstrated a 30% reduction in the incidence of major cardiovascular events in participants who followed a Mediterranean diet enriched with extra virgin olive oil or nuts.

This scientific data reinforces the points previously discussed, underscoring the cardiovascular benefits of the keto-Mediterranean diet.

However, it's essential to remember that diet is just one component of an overall healthy lifestyle. Regular physical activity, quality sleep, stress management, and regular health monitoring are just as important for maintaining a healthy heart. And, as always, changes to diet and lifestyle should be discussed and planned with a health professional to ensure they meet individual needs and health goals.

CHAPTER 12 The Keto-Mediterranean Diet and Mental Health: The Mind-Body Connection

The interconnection between the mind and body is no longer a topic of debate but a principle widely accepted in the field of medicine. The way we nourish our bodies can profoundly impact our mental well-being, and the keto-Mediterranean diet can play a fundamental role in this context.

While providing the body with adequate caloric intake, this diet emphasizes high-quality foods. These foods can nourish the brain, promote its proper functioning, and thus, enhance our mental health. Let's examine in detail how this happens.

Starting with healthy fats, a cornerstone of this diet, these nutrients are essential for brain health. The brain is composed of 60% fats, and to keep it healthy, it requires a steady intake of essential fatty acids, such as omega-3 and omega-6.

These fatty acids help maintain the integrity of cellular membranes, thereby influencing communication between nerve cells.

Moreover, they are vital for the formation of new neurons and synapses, key processes for learning and memory.

But it doesn't stop there. With its low carbohydrate intake, it can positively impact mood stability. Refined sugars, often present in large quantities in Western diets, cause sudden spikes and drops in blood glucose levels. This can lead to mood swings and feelings of irritability. Instead, this diet recommends limited carbohydrate consumption, favoring complex carbs with a low glycemic index, allowing a more consistent and gradual release of glucose into the blood.

Lastly, the nutrient richness of the keto-Mediterranean diet provides the brain with all the essential elements for optimal functioning. B vitamins, magnesium, zinc, iron, and antioxidants are just a few of the fundamental nutrients for brain health, all abundant in a keto-Mediterranean diet.

These are just some ways this diet can promote mental health.

The Keto-Mediterranean Diet and the Brain.

Our brain requires a significant amount of energy to function correctly, and the energy sources we choose can greatly affect its health. This nutrient-rich, low-carbohydrate diet provides the brain with the resources it needs for optimal performance.

One of the key benefits of this diet concerns cognitive function. Reducing carbohydrate intake and increasing healthy fat consumption helps stabilize blood sugar levels, leading to increased mental clarity and focus. Some research suggests a keto diet can even enhance cognitive functions in individuals with neurodegenerative diseases like Alzheimer's and Parkinson's.

Memory is another aspect of brain function that can benefit from this diet. Increased intake of Omega-3 fatty acids, found in foods like fish and olives, can support neuron function and structure, thus improving memory and learning. Additionally, the absence of sugar spikes in the blood can help prevent inflammation, which has been linked to memory loss and cognitive decline.

The nourishment from fruits, vegetables, fish, and olive oil, rich in antioxidants and phytonutrients, protects the brain from oxidative damage, helping maintain neuron health.

Some of these foods, like berries and spinach, also contain compounds that can help reduce brain inflammation.

A diet like the keto-Mediterranean, which promotes gut health through fiber and probiotics, may support better mental health due to the gut-brain connection.

And with this combination of nutritional principles, it has proven to offer several benefits for brain health, including improving cognitive function and memory.

Combining a healthy diet with other healthy lifestyle practices, such as adequate sleep and regular physical activity, can lead to even greater improvements in brain health.

The Keto-Mediterranean Diet and Mood.

The connection between what we eat and how we feel is increasingly recognized in the fields of nutrition and psychiatry. A diet providing the right balance of nutrients can have a potent effect on our mood and emotional well-being. Let's explore how the keto-Mediterranean diet may influence these aspects.

Firstly, it's essential to understand that our brain is primarily made up of fats. Hence, it's no surprise that an adequate intake of healthy fats, like those provided by the keto-Mediterranean diet, can support brain health and, consequently, mood. Specifically, Omega-3 fatty acids, found in foods like fish and olive oil, have shown positive effects on mood and depression.

Additionally, stabilizing blood sugar levels, a common result of adopting a keto dietary regimen, can help prevent the mood swings often associated with glucose fluctuations. Avoiding sudden spikes and drops in sugar can contribute to a sense of emotional balance and stability.

Another important aspect is the effect of diet on gut health. Numerous studies suggest a strong connection between the gut and brain, known as the gut-brain axis.

A healthy gut can produce a range of neurotransmitters and hormones that affect our mood, including serotonin, often dubbed the "happiness hormone". The keto-Mediterranean diet, rich in fiber and probiotics, can promote healthy gut flora, positively influencing mood and emotional well-being.

The Mediterranean diet has been linked to a lower incidence of depression in several studies. Although the exact reasons for this aren't entirely clear, it's believed that the high consumption of vegetables, fruits, fish, and olive oil, combined with the low presence of red meats and refined sugars, contributes to this positive effect.

This diet can significantly impact mood, potentially helping reduce symptoms of depression and anxiety. As always, it's important to note that if one is dealing with severe mental health issues, the diet can be just a part of the treatment plan, which must be supervised by a health professional.

The Keto-Mediterranean Diet and Sleep

Sleep is an essential aspect of our mental health. Proper nighttime rest can enhance mood, strengthen memory, boost creativity, and even help prevent diseases such as Alzheimer's. But how does the keto-Mediterranean diet affect sleep quality?

We know that food can have a significant impact on sleep. Consuming overly heavy or sugary foods can disrupt rest, while those rich in specific nutrients can promote it. In this respect, the nutritional principles offered by the keto-Mediterranean diet can provide various benefits.

One of the most significant benefits of the keto-Mediterranean regimen for sleep may come from stabilizing blood sugar levels. When sugar levels fluctuate overnight, our sleep can be interrupted. A low-carbohydrate diet like keto, combined with fiber-rich Mediterranean foods, can help keep glucose levels steady, facilitating a more restful sleep.

Typical Mediterranean diet foods, like fatty fish rich in omega-3 and almonds rich in magnesium, are known for their sleep benefits. Omega-3 can help regulate circadian rhythms, while magnesium can promote relaxation and the production of melatonin, the sleep hormone.

Furthermore, switching to fat metabolism for energy, typical of the keto regime, can affect sleep. Some research suggests that the keto diet might increase REM sleep, the sleep phase associated with dreaming and memory consolidation.

Another benefit of the Mediterranean diet encourages moderate consumption of red wine. Red wine contains melatonin, which can help regulate the sleep-wake cycle.

Despite these potential benefits, it's essential to remember that transitioning to a keto diet can initially cause sleep disturbances in some people, a phenomenon known as "keto flu." This effect tends to dissipate as the body adapts to the new diet.

In short, the keto-Mediterranean diet can offer various strategies to improve sleep quality, vital for mental health. As always, it's crucial to remember that diet is just one component of a healthy lifestyle and does not replace consultation with a health professional for specific issues.

At this point, we can reflect on the various ways the combination of nutritional principles present in the keto-Mediterranean mix can influence mental health. We've explored the potential impact of this dietary regime on brain function, mood, sleep, and now, we will focus on research findings in these areas.

On the cognitive front, a 2017 review published in the "Journal of Alzheimer's Disease" found that the keto diet could have protective effects against cognitive decline and neurodegenerative diseases. These benefits seem to come from the diet's ability to improve the brain's energy efficiency and reduce inflammation.

Regarding mood, a 2017 study published in the "Journal of Physiology - Paris" found that the keto diet might have antidepressant and anxiolytic effects in animals. Additionally, a comprehensive 2019 study published in the "Journal of Affective Disorders" discovered that adherence to the Mediterranean diet is associated with a reduced risk of depression in humans.

In terms of sleep, research is less definitive. Some studies have found improvements in sleep with the keto diet, while others have reported sleep disturbances, at least during the initial transition phase. It's clear that further research is needed to better understand these relationships.

While research is promising, it's crucial to remember that diet is only part of the mental health picture. Genetics, environment, lifestyle, and stress management all play significant roles. Moreover, while the keto-Mediterranean diet might have numerous benefits, it isn't suitable for everyone. Every individual is unique, and what works for one person may not work for another.

In essence, the relationship between food and the brain is an ever-evolving field of research. While scientific evidence suggests a promising link between the keto-Mediterranean combination and mental health, the key is a personalized approach. It's essential to work with a healthcare professional to develop a meal plan that respects individual needs and contributes to an overall sense of well-being.

CHAPTER 13 Sustainability and Adaptability: Making the Keto-Mediterranean Diet a Lifestyle

Good organization can make all the difference in the long-term success of any endeavor, and adopting a new diet is no exception. Introducing the keto-Mediterranean diet may require significant changes in daily eating habits, but careful planning can make this process much more manageable. One of the most effective ways to do this is meal planning. This practice involves planning in advance what you will eat for each meal and snack throughout the week. Meal planning can simplify shopping, ensure that you always have appropriate options available, and help avoid impulsive food decisions that may not align with the principles of the keto-Mediterranean diet.

In addition to planning weekly meals, it's also useful to have a 'basic' food list for the keto-Mediterranean diet handy. This list might include low-carb vegetables, fish and seafood, lean meats, nuts and seeds, and other key foods of the keto-Mediterranean diet. Having a checklist can make shopping simpler and ensure you always have the necessary ingredients to prepare meals.

Meal prepping is another strategy that can help maintain diet adherence. Preparing meals or meal components in advance can save time during the week and make it easier to stick to the diet even when busy. For example, you can cook large quantities of low-carb vegetables, lean proteins, or soups in advance and then store them in the fridge or freezer for future meals.

Planning might require some time at the beginning, but with practice, it can become an integral part of the routine. It not only can make adhering to the keto-Mediterranean diet easier but can also help reduce stress and increase confidence in one's ability to make healthy food choices. Remember, long-term success with the keto-Mediterranean diet is not about making perfect food choices, but a consistent commitment to making healthier choices most of the time.

Adaptability is a crucial aspect of the keto-Mediterranean diet, underlining its effectiveness and longevity. Unlike many other diets, it is not about strict dietary regimens or set rules but rather a dietary philosophy that can be shaped based on individual needs. This lies primarily in the fact that it allows a broad range of food options. Despite its guidelines, the diet includes a wide variety of foods, allowing plenty of room for experimentation and personalization.

This means if a particular food doesn't suit your taste or nutritional goals, many alternatives are available.

Another key element concerns the pace and approach to transitioning into this diet. There's no need to immediately switch to a strict keto regimen; the transition can occur gradually, allowing the body to adjust to the changes and learn to use fat reserves as the primary energy source.

Adaptability also extends to managing special occasions and temptations. For instance, occasionally indulging in a carb-rich dish or dessert is possible without feeling like the entire journey has been compromised. The key is to get back to the keto-Mediterranean diet regimen and continue to make it a lifestyle, which is a major factor promoting its long-term sustainability. It offers the flexibility needed to navigate daily challenges and allows each of us to adapt the diet based on our unique needs, making it a healthy and viable lifestyle option.

Adopting a new diet, especially one as distinct as the keto-Mediterranean diet, isn't always a straightforward and linear journey. There can be challenges along the way, but recognizing and preparing for them is integral to success.

A common challenge might be the so-called "keto-flu", or the ketosis adaptation syndrome.

This is a brief period during which your body adjusts to the switch from using carbohydrates to fats as the primary energy source. During this phase, you may experience symptoms like fatigue, headaches, or irritability. It's essential to remember that this is a temporary phase, and several ways exist to mitigate the symptoms, such as ensuring ample water intake, consuming adequate mineral salts, and getting enough sleep.

Another challenge can be managing temptations and social situations. Dining out or attending social events can present difficulties, as not all restaurants or social occasions will offer keto-friendly options. However, with some planning and strategy, these situations can be managed. You might consider eating a keto-compatible meal before attending an event or bringing keto-compatible snacks with you.

Additionally, it's crucial to recognize that there will be days when you're not perfect - and that's okay. The important thing is not to view these moments as failures but as parts of a journey. Remember that each day is an opportunity to make healthier choices.

Remember, support is vital. Reach out to your community, whether it's friends, family, or online groups of people following the same diet. Sharing your challenges and successes can be extremely motivating.

Challenges may arise along the way, but with the right mindset and suitable strategies, they can be overcome, making the keto-Mediterranean diet a genuinely sustainable lifestyle.

In a world where environmental sustainability is increasingly at the forefront of discussion, how can the keto-Mediterranean diet fit into this new paradigm? The answer lies in the combination of ketogenic and Mediterranean principles. The latter emphasizes the use of fresh, local, and seasonal products, an approach that benefits not only our health but also the environment.

Using local and seasonal ingredients means reducing our food's carbon footprint. Less distance between the field and our table results in fewer greenhouse gas emissions from food transportation. At the same time, eating seasonal foods contributes to crop diversity, preserving soil health, and reducing the need for chemical fertilizers.

Another aspect to consider is the choice of protein sources. While the ketogenic diet emphasizes proteins, the keto-Mediterranean version encourages a higher consumption of fish over red meat.

This not only has health benefits but also a lesser environmental impact, as meat production, especially beef, is one of the largest contributors to greenhouse gas emissions.

Moreover, it's important to remember that despite its focus on fats, the keto-Mediterranean diet promotes the intake of healthy fats from plant-based sources such as olive oil, nuts, and seeds. These foods are not only nutritious, but their production also has a much lower environmental impact compared to fats of animal origin.

The adaptability of the keto-Mediterranean diet allows for easily incorporating sustainability principles. You can choose organic foods, opt for recyclable packaging, or minimize food waste, for example, by using leftovers for subsequent meals.

When followed with awareness and care, this diet can not only support our health but also contribute to a healthier and more sustainable environment.

We have delved into various aspects of the keto-Mediterranean diet, showing how it can contribute to our physical and mental health and overall well-being. However, it is important to note that all these benefits can only be achieved and maintained if the keto-Mediterranean diet becomes a way of life and not a quick or temporary solution.

Adopting the keto-Mediterranean diet as a lifestyle doesn't mean following strict and inflexible rules. On the contrary, it's about embracing a balanced and moderate food approach that encourages variety, quality, and the enjoyment of food. It also means understanding that there isn't a one-size-fits-all solution, but rather a set of principles and guidelines to adapt to our unique needs, tastes, and lifestyles.

An integral part of this dietary approach is listening to one's body. Sometimes, in trying to follow a diet or specific food plan, we can lose connection with our body's signals. However, paying attention to our hunger and fullness, noticing how our body feels after eating certain foods, can be a powerful tool to guide our food choices and create a sustainable and satisfying eating pattern.

We also emphasize the importance of a holistic approach to health and well-being. While nutrition plays a crucial role in our health, it's just a piece of the puzzle. Other elements like regular physical exercise, adequate sleep, stress management, and positive social relationships are equally important. Adopting the keto-Mediterranean diet as a lifestyle means integrating these various elements into a comprehensive approach to well-being.

In conclusion, we invite you to see the keto-Mediterranean diet as a journey, a continuous exploration, and experimentation. It's a path that can enrich not only our health but also our relationship with food, our bodies, and the world around us. Remember, the journey to well-being is just that, a journey, and like all journeys, it's best to enjoy the journey itself, not just the destination.

And so, we come to the end of this journey. A journey of discovery into a new way of seeing food and health, which allowed us to explore the power of the keto-Mediterranean diet. Along the way, we learned that the real key to well-being isn't about rigidly adhering to a diet but embracing a balanced and mindful lifestyle, where diet harmonizes with exercise, rest, and mental activity.

We have explored the different facets of this dietary approach, from the benefits for physical and mental health, environmental sustainability, to strategies for tackling challenges and obstacles along the way. However, our most significant discovery might be the importance of listening to our body, respecting its needs, and signals.

As you take your first steps or continue your journey towards greater well-being, remember that you are not alone. There are resources, people, and communities out there that can support you. This book has been a first step, a guide to light the way, but the road ahead is still long and full of discoveries.

I hope these pages have inspired you to embark on or continue your journey toward a healthier and happier life. Remember, the key is to embrace the keto-Mediterranean diet not just as a mere dietary regime, but as a lifestyle: a sustainable and healthy way of living that allows you to fully enjoy food and life.

And so, we close with a wish: may the journey towards health and well-being be for you a path illuminated with discoveries, satisfaction, and joy. As the Spanish writer Miguel de Cervantes said, "The journey is better than the inn." Safe travels and good life to all!

MIA BREEZE

Here's a gift for YOU.

This daily journal is a gift from me to always keep your days at their best and to thank you once again.

How to Download the Extra Gift:

- Find the QR code below.
- Open the camera on your smartphone or tablet and scan the QR code. Most devices will automatically recognize the code.
- Tap the link that appears on your device screen to open the recipe book.
- Immediately download your daily journal to your device!

Printed in Great Britain
by Amazon